From Equity Insights to Action

We dedicate this book to the unparalleled talents, gifts, and spirits of multilingual learners and their teachers.

We also dedicate this book to our respective families, who are our daily inspirations:

Howie, Benjamin, Jacob, and Noah (Andrea)

Tim, Dave, Jason, Sara, Christine, Meadow, Gavin, and Rohnan (Maria)

Susan Feinsilver Thomas, my sister (Audrey)

Mell, Justin, Taylor, and Nicole (Carrie)

From Equity Insights to Action

Critical Strategies for Teaching Multilingual Learners

Andrea Honigsfeld

Maria G. Dove

Audrey Cohan

Carrie McDermott Goldman

Illustrated by Claribel González

FOR INFORMATION:

Corwin

A SAGE Company

2455 Teller Road

Thousand Oaks, California 91320

(800) 233-9936

www.corwin.com

SAGE Publications Ltd.

1 Oliver's Yard

55 City Road

London EC1Y 1SP

United Kingdom

SAGE Publications India Pvt. Ltd.

B 1/I 1 Mohan Cooperative Industrial Area

Mathura Road, New Delhi 110 044

India

SAGE Publications Asia-Pacific Pte. Ltd.

18 Cross Street #10-10/11/12

China Square Central

Singapore 048423

President: Mike Soules

Associate Vice President and
  Editorial Director: Monica Eckman

Program Director and Publisher: Dan Alpert

Senior Content Development Editor: Lucas Schleicher

Associate Content Development Editor: Mia Rodriguez

Editorial Development Manager: Julie Nemer

Project Editor: Amy Schroller

Copy Editor: Karin Rathert

Typesetter: C&M Digitals (P) Ltd.

Proofreader: Dennis Webb

Indexer: Sheila Hill

Cover Designer: Candice Harman

Marketing Manager: Sharon Pendergast

Library of Congress Cataloging-in-Publication Data

Names: Honigsfeld, Andrea, 1965- author. | Dove, Maria G., author. | Cohan, Audrey, author. | Goldman, Carrie McDermott, author.

Title: From equity insights to action : critical strategies for teaching multilingual learners / Andrea Honigsfeld, Maria G. Dove, Audrey Cohan, Carrie McDermott Goldman ; Illustrated by Claribel González.

Description: Thousand Oaks, California : Corwin, [2022] | Includes bibliographical references and index.

Identifiers: LCCN 2021026874 | ISBN 9781071855065 (paperback) | ISBN 9781071855058 (epub) | ISBN 9781071855041 (epub) | ISBN 9781071855034 (pdf)

Subjects: LCSH: Educational equalization. | English language—Study and teaching—Foreign speakers—Social aspects. | Multilingualism in children. | Mulitcultural education.

Classification: LCC LC213 .H66 2022 | DDC 379.2/6—dc23

LC record available at https://lccn.loc.gov/2021026874

This book is printed on acid-free paper.

21 22 23 24 25 10 9 8 7 6 5 4 3 2 1

Contents

Acknowledgments

This project would not have been possible without the creative inspiration and support of Dan Alpert, publisher and program director, our beloved editor and mentor extraordinaire and unmatched champion of equity. It is with heartfelt appreciation that we recognize this book might have never been written—especially with an accelerated timeline and ready for the fall of 2021—if Dan did not recognize our passion for sharing our hopes and equitable strategies for multilingual learners. It is with great enthusiasm that we also applaud the efforts of Lucas Schleicher, senior content development editor, and Mia Rodriguez, associate content development editor at Corwin Press, and Rose Storey, art director at SAGE, who all worked together and brought this book to fruition. We would also like to thank the entire Corwin Press team for guiding the production of this book every step of the way and giving us the opportunity to share our voices.

We wish to acknowledge the extraordinary talent and patience of Claribel González, who provided the most stunning sketchnotes that open each chapter.

There are many educators to thank as well! We asked teachers around the United States and beyond to respond to a series of open-ended, anonymous survey questions a few months ago and we were sincerely moved by the overwhelming response. To continue the dialogue, we invited those who shared their names and emails with us and volunteered to join us for a handful of optional Zoom focus group discussions. We are forever indebted to your generosity for sharing your successes and challenges, your brilliance and compassion, and for your encouragement to get this book out for the new academic year! We wish to acknowledge how you directly or indirectly contributed to this book by inspiring us, affirming our thinking, or giving us permission to incorporate your ideas in this book:

Caryn Bachar, ENL lead teacher, Hewlett-Woodmere Schools, New York

Brianna Carnevale, ENL teacher, Long Beach Public Schools, New York

Elizabeth Choi, ELL teacher, Knox County Schools, Tennessee

Evelyn Daza, ENL director, Long Beach School District, New York

Diana Delaney, Title III newcomer support specialist, Forsyth County School, Georgia

Andrea Dell'Olio, ENL teacher, New York City Department of Education, New York

Elena Dokshansky, ENL teacher, Buffalo Public Schools, and adjunct professor, Buffalo State College, New York

Mariel Gomez de la Torre-Cerfontaine, ESL teacher, Rowan Salisbury Schools, North Carolina

Yuriko Gray, ENL teacher and coordinator, New York City Department of Education, New York

Josephine Hall, ENL teacher, Westbury Public Schools, New York

Tan Huynh, MYP individuals & societies teacher, KIS International School, Bangkok, Thailand

Nadia Khan-Roopnarine, English teacher, New York City Department of Education, New York

Soula Katsogianopoulos, ELL project lead, Council of Directors of Education (CODE), Ontario, Canada

Bailey K. Ledesma, science and EL coordinator, Waikiki Elementary School, Hawaii

Sherry Liptak, district ELL specialist, Chilliwack School District #33, British Columbia, Canada

Nancy Lopes, ENL teacher, Commack School District, New York

Meghan Lydon, ELL teacher, Casablanca American School, Morocco

Jody Nolf, ESOL coordinator, Palm Beach County School District, Florida

Mary Sandoval, ENL teacher leader, Guilderland Central School District, New York

Beth Skelton, U.S. and international consultant, Colorado

We would like to express our most sincere appreciation to our critical friends who read earlier drafts of select chapters or excerpts of this book and offered feedback and affirmation (often within days to stay on track with our timeline). Your wisdom, vast professional expertise, and critical insights only made this book so much better, all errors that remain are ours.

Dr. Margo Gottlieb, co-founder and lead developer, WIDA at the Wisconsin Center for Education Research, Wisconsin, author, Corwin Press

Alycia Owen, MS/HS EAL teacher, head of department, American International School of Guangzhou, China

Kristina Robertson, English learner (EL) program administrator, Roseville Public Schools, Minnesota

Dr. Paul Romanelli, assistant superintendent for curriculum and instruction, Long Beach School District, New York

Lindsey Rose, director of languages, North Shore School District 112, Illinois

Dr. Ivannia Soto, professor of education and director of graduate programs at Whittier College, California, author, Corwin Press

Dr. Katie Toppel, English language development specialist, Tigard-Tualatin School District, Oregon

Ron D. Woo, executive director, NYS Language RBERN, Metropolitan Center at New York University, New York

Finally, we wish to acknowledge you, the readers of this book! You inspired us to get up early or stay up late, call, text, Zoom, and email each other at all hours of the day to keep writing, editing, polishing, and revising this book until it was ready to be released!

About the Authors

Andrea Honigsfeld, EdD, is associate dean and professor in the School of Education and Human Services at Molloy College, Rockville Centre, New York. She directs a doctoral program in Educational Leadership for Diverse Learning Communities. Before entering the field of higher education, she was an English-as-a-foreign-language teacher in Hungary (Grades 5–8 and adult) and an English-as-a-second-language teacher in New York City (Grades K–3 and adult). She also taught Hungarian at New York University.

She was the recipient of a doctoral fellowship at St. John's University, New York, where she conducted research on individualized instruction and learning styles. She has published extensively on working with English language learners and providing individualized instruction based on learning style preferences. She received a Fulbright Award to lecture in Iceland in the fall of 2002. In the past 18 years, she has been presenting at conferences across the United States, Great Britain, Denmark, Sweden, the Philippines, and the United Arab Emirates. She frequently offers staff development, primarily focusing on effective differentiated strategies and collaborative practices for English-as-a-second-language and general-education teachers. She coauthored *Differentiated Instruction for At-Risk Students* (2009) and coedited the five-volume Breaking the Mold of Education series (2010–2013), published by Rowman and Littlefield. She is also the coauthor of *Core Instructional Routines: Go-To Structures for Effective Literacy Teaching, K–5 and 6–12* (2014) and author of *Growing Language and Literacy* (2019), published by Heinemann. With Maria Dove, she coedited *Coteaching and Other Collaborative Practices in the EFL/ESL Classroom: Rationale, Research, Reflections, and Recommendations* (2012) and *Co-Teaching for English Learners: Evidence-based Practices and Research-Informed Outcomes* (2020). Maria and Andrea also coauthored *Collaboration and Co-Teaching: Strategies for English Learners* (2010), *Common Core for the Not-So-Common Learner,*

Grades K–5: English Language Arts Strategies (2013), *Common Core for the Not-So-Common Learner, Grades 6–12: English Language Arts Strategies* (2013), *Beyond Core Expectations: A Schoolwide Framework for Serving the Not-So-Common Learner* (2014), *Collaboration and Co-Teaching: A Leader's Guide* (2015), *Coteaching for English Learners: A Guide to Collaborative Planning, Instruction, Assessment, and Reflection* (2018), and *Collaborating for English Learners: A Foundational Guide to Integrated Practices* (2019), seven of which are Corwin bestsellers. She is a contributing author of *Breaking Down the Wall: Essential Shifts for English Learner Success* (2020).

Maria G. Dove, EdD, is a professor in the School of Education and Human Services at Molloy College, Rockville Centre, New York. She teaches preservice and inservice teachers about the research and best practices for implementing effective instruction for English learners, and she supports doctoral students in the EdD program in Educational Leadership for Diverse Learning Communities. Before entering the field of higher education, she worked for over thirty years as an English-as-a-second-language teacher in public school settings (Grades K–12) and in adult English language programs in the greater New York City area. She frequently provides professional development for educators throughout the United States on the teaching of multilingual learners. She also serves as a mentor for new ESOL teachers as well as an instructional coach for general-education teachers and literacy specialists.

With Andrea Honigsfeld, she has coauthored multiple best-selling Corwin books, including *Collaboration and Co-Teaching: Strategies for English Learners* (2010), *Common Core for the Not-So-Common Learner, Grades K–5: English Language Arts Strategies* (2013), and *Common Core for the Not-So-Common Learner, Grades 6–12: English Language Arts Strategies* (2013), *Collaboration and Co-Teaching: A Leader's Guide* (2015), *Co-Teaching for English Learners: A Guide to Collaborative Planning, Instruction, Assessment, and Reflection* (2018). Along with other Corwin top-named authors, she coauthored *Breaking Down the Wall: Essential Shifts for English Learner Success* (2020). In addition, she coedited, *Coteaching and Other Collaborative Practices in the EFL/ESL Classroom: Rationale, Research, Reflections, and Recommendations* (2012) and *Co-Teaching for English Learners: Evidence-based Practices and Research-Informed Outcomes* (2020) published by Information Age. With Audrey Cohan and Andrea Honigsfeld, she coauthored *Beyond Core Expectations: A Schoolwide Framework for Serving the*

Not-So-Common Learner (2014), published by Corwin, and *Team Up, Speak Up, Fire Up!: Educators, Students, and the Community Working Together to Support English Learners* (2020), published by ASCD.

 **Audrey Cohan**, EdD, is the senior dean for research and scholarship at Molloy College, Rockville Centre, New York. She has been at Molloy College for twenty-six years, during which time she served as professor, chairperson of the Education Department, and interim dean for the Division of Natural Sciences. Dr. Cohan has taught in the undergraduate and graduate programs and is currently teaching Critical Issues at the doctoral level for the EdD program, Leadership for Diverse Learning Communities.

She began her career as a special education teacher in New York City working with students with special needs in both self-contained and resource room settings. Her first book was published in 1995 titled *Sexual Harassment and Sexual Abuse: A Handbook for Teachers and Administrators*. This coauthored book was an outgrowth of her dissertation work, which focused on child sexual abuse within schools. Dr. Cohan coedited a five-volume Breaking the Mold of Education series about educational innovation with Dr. Andrea Honigsfeld. She has published numerous peer-reviewed articles about English language learners including "Differentiating Between Learning Disabilities and Typical Second Language Acquisition: A Case Study" and "Piloting a Pre-referral Data Collection Tool: A Documentary Account," as she has New York State certification in special education and TESOL. The textbook published in 2016, *Serving English Language Learners*, earned the Textbook & Academic Authors Association (TAA) Most Promising New Textbook Award. Her other coauthored book publications include *Beyond Core Expectations: A Schoolwide Framework for Serving the Not-So-Common Learner* (2014), *America's Peace-Minded Educator: John Dewey* (2016), and *Team Up, Speak Up, Fire Up!: Educators, Students, and the Community Working Together to Support English Learners* (2020). Dr. Cohan is also the principal investigator of a National Science Foundation (NSF) Robert Noyce grant for $1,450,000, which is designed to recruit bilingual STEM teachers for high-needs schools. While at Molloy College, Dr. Cohan has been the recipient of the Faculty Leadership Award, the Faculty Recognition Award, the Research Award, and the Distinguished Service Award.

Carrie McDermott Goldman, EdD, is associate professor, coordinator of graduate and post-graduate TESOL/bilingual programs, and director of bilingual and TESOL grants at Molloy College, Rockville Centre, New York. She teaches preservice and inservice teachers equitable pedagogical approaches, research- and asset-based practices, and embedded language theory. Prior to higher education, she taught preK–12 in high-needs settings and college-level ESL. She continues to collaborate with schools as an instructional coach and mentor for teachers and administrators. Throughout the pandemic, she also created and implemented an online teaching mentoring program.

She is involved in several projects. She coauthored and serves as the director and principal investigator for the New York State Grant for the U.S. Department of Education, *Clinically Rich Intensive Teachers Institute in Bilingual Education and TESOL (CR-ITI BE/ESOL)* for $550,000 over five years to meet the growing needs of MLLs throughout the region. Her most recent works include, "Co-Taught Integrated Language and Mathematics Content Instruction for Multilingual Learners," a coauthored chapter with Andrea Honigsfeld in *Effective Teacher Collaboration for English Language Learners: Cross-Curricular Insights From K–12 Classrooms* (Yoon, Ed., 2021); "Positive Outcomes for ELs in an Integrated Social Studies Class," coauthored with Andrea Honigsfeld in *Co-Teaching for English Learners: Evidence-based Practices and Research-Informed Outcomes* (Dove & Honigsfeld, Eds., 2020); "Classroom Management for Culturally and Linguistically Diverse Learners," coauthored with Lisa Peluso in *Approaches to Classroom Management for Diverse and Inclusive Schools* (Alcruz & Blair, Eds., in press); "Preparing Social Studies and ESOL Teachers for Integrated Language and Content Instruction in Support of ELLs," with Andrea Honigsfeld and Kelley Cordeiro in *Teaching History and Social Studies to English Language Learners: Preparing Pre-service and In-service Teachers* (de Oliveira & Obenchain, Eds., 2018); "Preparing Science Teachers for Project-based, Integrated, Collaborative Instruction," coauthored with Andrea Honigsfeld in *Teaching Science to English Language Learners: Preparing Pre-service and In-service Teachers* (de Oliveira & Campbell Wilcox, Eds., 2017); and "Culturally Responsive Teaching in a Secondary, Integrated Mathematics Class" (2021), in *New York State ASCD Impact Journal*.

About the Illustrator

Claribel González, EdM, is a staff developer in western New York. She supports administrators, teachers, and other stakeholders in achieving academic excellence for multilingual learners. Her passion for language and equity started at a young age as a result of her participation in bilingual and ESL programs. As an avid doodler, she celebrates creativity and the power of sketchnotes as a vehicle to synthesize information. Claribel has also served as a bilingual classroom teacher and instructional coach.

Establish Your Why

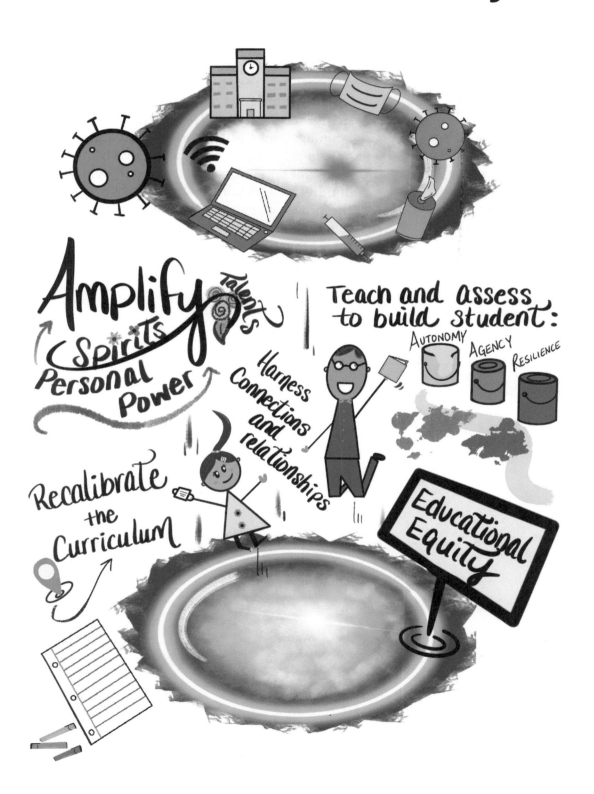

We are writing this book in April 2021; right around the corner is the summer break, and then the new academic year will begin. We are anxiously awaiting good news about the impact of the COVID-19 vaccinations and anticipating the drop in infection rates; we are eagerly watching how the Biden-Harris administration is enacting policies that address long-standing yet pressing societal ills such as racism, discrimination, and socioeconomic divides head-on; and we are looking forward to new beginnings as we hope to see all of our students and their teachers return to schools without fear and with newfound energy and purpose.

But we pause to recognize the power of this moment, the interconnectedness of our past, present, and future. And we note that a portal has opened, creating a pathway between the past and the future. The portal metaphor we are borrowing comes from renowned Indian novelist Arundhati Roy (2020), who reflected on the dire needs in her homeland when she wrote:

> *Historically, pandemics have forced humans to break with the past and imagine their world anew. This one is no different. It is a portal, a gateway between one world and the next. We can choose to walk through it, dragging the carcasses of our prejudice and hatred, our avarice, our data banks and dead ideas, our dead rivers and smoky skies behind us. Or we can walk through lightly, with little luggage, ready to imagine another world. And ready to fight for it.* (para. 58)

The portal metaphor offers you an invitation to enter this chapter and book and to envision educational equity for multilingual learners (MLs) at a rare moment in history. While metaphors are contextual and often culturally bound, we believe that a portal has opened for all of us. Like Arundhati Roy's powerful claim, our *educational equity portal* metaphor also invites us to consider the gateway between the educational world we knew before the pandemic and the next one we are ready to create. We can enter the portal dragging generations of inequities, injustices, prejudices and biases, and deficit-based and damage-centered thinking and actions with us. Or we can walk through the portal ready to imagine and fight for a world of equity in our classrooms, schools, and communities. What do we take with us? What do we leave behind? And how do we start again? What do we need to urgently change in our daily practice? It is up to each of us! Our intent with this book is to offer guidance and practical strategies on how to navigate this portal.

THE URGENCY

"Let's shift from empowering our multilingual students to creating opportunities for them to thrive by using the curriculum and instruction as a vehicle that sustains their cultural and linguistic connections. That's how we can best support them!"

—Tan Huynh

Our research and advocacy work in educator support regarding equity for MLs is not new; yet, the urgency to write this book right now is! This book is not about the pandemic, but we have to recognize the context in which equity must be front and center in every conversation and action we take for so many reasons. At this point, as we are living history, we would like to invite all educators to reflect on why we must seize this moment to start anew and make the following commitments:

1. Together, let's challenge the notions of a learning loss, pandemic slow down, or a COVID slide because they create or reinforce a deficit mindset, which in turn, may result in falling back on perpetual cycles of remediation and interventions for many of our MLs and other vulnerable students. Instead, we call for equitable opportunities for MLs that begin with recognizing their strengths, abilities, and talents; that engage them to contribute to curricula that are culturally, historically, and linguistically responsive and sustaining; and that ultimately draw them to partake in instruction using multimodal and multilingual representations and nonlinguistic expressions so that MLs have full ownership of their academic, linguistic, and social-emotional growth.

2. Together, let's challenge the notions of going back to normal, accepting the pre-pandemic curricular and instructional practices, inequities, and more. Instead, we call for critically re-examining our current beliefs and practices and setting clearer pathways, better protocols, equitable learning opportunities for MLs to fully develop their agency and autonomy, to be recognized as bilingual and biliterate or multilingual and multiliterate future leaders.

3. Together, let's challenge the notions of defining MLs by labels, describing them as struggling readers and writers, at-risk students, or slow learners who cannot seem to close the achievement gap. Instead, we call for equitable opportunities for MLs to tap into their identities, interests, and cultural, familial, and individual knowledge and use all their gifts, talents, rich cultural backgrounds, full linguistic repertoires, as well as newfound skills and competencies.

Before you move through the portal with us, stop and critically reflect on your beliefs:

- What beliefs do you need to challenge in your context?

- What additional equitable opportunities do MLs urgently need?

- What special gifts and talents do they offer to your classroom and school community?

- What drives you to pursue equity in your daily work or what is your *why*?

It is time to reimagine and recommit to equity for MLs. If not now, then when?

WHO ARE MULTILINGUAL LEARNERS?

When we refer to multilingual learners, we mean all school-age children and youngsters in the United States and beyond who live in multilingual communities, experience the world through multiple languages, and interact in one or more languages other than English, whether they are classified as English learners or participate in English language development or bilingual programs or not. Multilingual families and their children are often at the intersectionality of race, ethnicity, socioeconomic status, and language, with the majority of MLs in the United States being non-white and speaking Spanish. We do not intend to silo this group or any groups of students within the context of any classroom or school. Just the opposite! What we learned from the National Equity Project (n.d.) is that by virtue of taking a broadened, larger-scale *focal student approach*, we can develop equity practices centering on select students yet ultimately impact a much larger student population. Our intention with this book is to demonstrate that understanding deeply what MLs experience, what assets and strengths they bring to our schools, and what they need to thrive will shift classroom practices for all students.

WHAT IS EQUITY?

Recently, more than ever before, equity has been the focus of conversations and concerted efforts in many ways. For our purposes, we offer the following succinct yet impactful definition of equity within the educational context: Equity is when every student gets what they need to live and learn to their fullest potential. More specifically, equity for multilingual learners means that their cultural and linguistic identities, backgrounds, and experiences are recognized as valued, rich sources of knowledge, and their academic, linguistic, literacy, and social-emotional growth is ensured to their fullest potential.

Equity work is multilayered and complex; it reaches far beyond what a single book can achieve. The structural inequities that permeate our society reflect a long, terrible history of social, economic, and educational injustice. We are fully aware that achieving equity is not a one-and-done effort; it is not a quick checklist, workshop, or an afterschool task delegated to a designated DEI (diversity, equity, and inclusion) person or committee in the school. It is hard work that necessitates a great deal of focus, time, and resources! While we are deeply committed to disrupting systemic racism, inequities, and discrimination and engaging in sustained equity work in and outside schools, the focus of this book is *students* and *teachers*. More specifically, we are here to address the urgent need to create equitable learning spaces (inside and outside classrooms) for MLs and to support teachers in their day-to-day quest to transform education for their students. We fully embrace Safir and Dugan's (2021) call for advocacy:

> "Equity isn't a destination but an unwavering commitment to a journey. It can be easy to focus on where we hope to land and lose sight of the deliberate daily actions that constitute the process" (p. 29).

In this book, we intend to stay focused on the deliberate daily actions that all teachers of multilingual learners can take. As part of sustained efforts that require systemic change, we must begin by examining our own identities and biases, identifying actionable daily practices that dismantle academic and linguistic barriers, and evaluating the impact of our actions. Inspired by Law and Robertson's (2021) *Five-Step ABCDE Leadership Equity Moves*, we invite you to establish *why* this work is needed in your context by committing to these equity practices.

Before introducing our approach to equity, stop and critically reflect on how others define equity:

Which of these definitions resonate with you the most and why? How do you and others in your school community define equity for students? Why it is important to develop clarity and shared ownership of what equity work is about?

"Educational equity means that every child receives whatever she/he/they need to develop to her/his/their full academic and social potential and to thrive, every day" (Aguilar, 2021, p. 6).

"Equity is an approach to ensuring equally high outcomes for all by removing the predictability of success or failure that currently correlates with any racial, social, economic, or cultural factor" (Safir & Dugan, 2021, p. 29).

"Public schools should provide equitable access and ensure all students have the knowledge and skills to succeed as contributing members of a rapidly changing global society, regardless of factors such as race, gender, sexual orientation, ethnic background, English proficiency, immigration status, socioeconomic status, or disability" (Center for Public Education, 2016, p. 2).

"Educational equity means that all students have the same access to educational success. It means using research-based/evidence-based instructional strategies and interventions that support student learning and mitigate student poverty and language background, and by creating stronger bridges between community health and social services and the schools. It also means developing a network of schools and districts that go beyond the status quo or the new normal to become models for others" (Zacarian et al., 2021, p. 133).

Take a moment and reflect whether you regularly and intentionally do the following:

Assess examples of inequities and their sources in your classroom

Build your capacity to get to know your students

Collaborate and communicate with students, families, and fellow educators

Determine your daily equity moves and actions

Evaluate your impact on students' academic, linguistic, and social-emotional development

While we have previously recognized that equity work is not limited to any subgroup of historically marginalized students, in this book we pay special attention to multilingual learners with their limitless potential and refuse any perceived linguistic and cultural barriers that are sometimes associated with this group. Which of these perpetual untruths and unfounded complaints have you heard about MLs?

- *He can't be in my advanced math class until he learns English.*

- *Her writing is impossible to read; it is full of grammatical and spelling errors!*

- *These kids miss a lot of days and seem to be late for class all the time.*

- *Something is wrong with that child. He does not speak any English even though he has been here for three months.*

- *Why do those girls always sit in the back of the classroom together and not pay attention to the lesson?*

- *They just aren't motivated to learn.*

- *These parents don't care about their child's education.*

Such misinformed views must be left behind and eradicated from our belief systems as we cross the portal that opened for us! They hurt our multilingual children and their families; they dismiss the multiple gifts they bring to our classrooms; they prevent us from seeing the children as they truly are with their assets and talents; and they are destructive and unacceptable. Instead, let's invoke the traditional Masai greeting, *"And how are the children?"* the customary answer to which is *"All the children are well!"* indicating that the most vulnerable part of the population is cared for no matter what is going on in the world (O'Neill, n.d.). On the other side of the pandemic, what would happen if we were guided by this type of greeting and insisted on sincere responses to it? How would we change our daily planning, instructional and assessment practices, as well as our own continued learning to be better at our craft if we had to reflect on this question every time we arrive for work early in the morning, pass a colleague in the hallway, enter the teachers' lounge for a short break, begin a parent-teacher conference, or when we leave for home at the end of the day?

HOW THIS BOOK GUIDES EQUITY WORK FOR MLS

To pass through the portal with our multilingual learners to post-pandemic times, teachers must share the belief that achieving equity is nonnegotiable. We are not going back to "normal," so let's collectively reject the status quo; instead, let's forge ahead and proceed with all our work with MLs through an equity lens. Our book will address the major teaching and learning challenges of returning to school by presenting equity-informed in support of MLs—one chapter at a time.

CHAPTER 1: ESTABLISH YOUR WHY

In this opening chapter, we use the portal as a metaphor for entering a new era and leaving the pandemic behind. We will recognize the disproportionate health, safety, and socioeconomic impact and psychosocial trauma COVID-19 had on disenfranchised communities. We offer an overall vision for meeting the needs of MLs by placing equity in focus and introducing four essential practices for equity on the other side of the pandemic for the sake of multilingual learner populations. MLs include English learners, bilingual- and dual-language learners, heritage language learners, and all students who have access to and utilize more than one linguistic system. We are determined to make a compelling case as to why teachers should engage in these practices and create equitable learning environments for their students in support of their academic, linguistic, literacy, and social-emotional learning growth. The four practices are:

1. Amplify the Talents, Spirits, and Personal Powers of MLs

2. Recalibrate the Curriculum to Accelerate Learning for MLs

3. Teach and Assess to Build Student Autonomy, Agency, and Resilience

4. Harness the Power of Connections and Relationships

CHAPTER 2: AMPLIFY THE TALENTS, SPIRITS, AND PERSONAL POWERS OF MLS

In the second chapter, we use a garden metaphor to depict the diversity among MLs and capture the rich and complex experiences culturally and linguistically diverse students bring to our classrooms and school communities. Let's get to know our students so they can truly amplify their talents, spirits, and personal powers. We challenge our readers to move beyond engaging MLs in previously established, typical academic learning and language and literacy development experiences; instead, we advocate for MLs to continue their journey to becoming independent, self-directed learners by recognizing, celebrating, and building on their many talents, passions, and special interests as well as their pandemic experiences of autonomy, decision-making, and independence.

CHAPTER 3: RECALIBRATE THE CURRICULUM TO ACCELERATE LEARNING FOR MLS

The third chapter examines what is currently in the curriculum and what should be in the curriculum for MLs. In this chapter, we use a GPS metaphor indicating that there are multiple pathways to the same destination. In light of the pandemic, we reject the notion of the frequently cited "learning loss" and instead argue for replacing remediation and deficit-thinking with acceleration and opportunities for students and teachers to co-create authentic curricula that are relevant, rigorous, and relational. Additional curriculum work highlighted in the chapter includes decolonizing, revising, and recalibrating curriculum that integrates content, language, and literacy development. Borrowing from Bishop's (1990) original idea of books becoming windows, mirrors, and sliding doors, we present how curricula across all content areas may be perceived similarly:

> Books are sometimes windows, offering views of worlds that may be real or imagined, familiar or strange. These windows are also sliding glass doors, and readers have only to walk through in imagination to become part of whatever world has been created or recreated by the author. When lighting conditions are just right, however, a window can also be a mirror. Literature transforms human experience and reflects it back to us, and in that reflection, we can see our own lives and experiences as part of a larger human experience. Reading, then, becomes a means of self-affirmation, and readers often seek their mirrors in books. (p. ix)

CHAPTER 4: TEACH AND ASSESS TO BUILD STUDENT AUTONOMY, AGENCY, AND RESILIENCE

The pandemic challenged our students and their teachers in unfathomable ways. The lessons learned in the past year need not go to waste! This chapter will use an artist's palette and toolkit as a metaphor to richly illustrate how we can recognize the ways students engage in the world and how they learn. This transformative approach to teaching and assessing fosters student autonomy, agency, and resilience through multidimensional instructional strategies and an equitable approach to assessment *as* and *for* learning. Special attention will be paid to integrating content, language, literacy, and social-emotional dimensions of learning.

CHAPTER 5: HARNESS THE POWER OF CONNECTIONS AND RELATIONSHIPS

In the final chapter, we broaden our perspective and examine ways equity must be a part of efforts inside and outside the classroom, across the entire school community, and beyond. We employ an ecosystem metaphor to capture the dynamic nature of creating a strong sense of classroom community, belonging, and purpose, supporting students' social-emotional well-being and freedom of expression, harnessing the system of social workers, guidance counselors, teaching aids, and others to offer mentoring and coaching as needed.

In Figure 1.1, we summarize the four key equity strategies for MLs and offer our *"whys"* in two ways—what is the purpose of the strategy (rationale) and why it matters (importance). Later in the chapter, we will invite you to establish your *whys* as well.

FIGURE 1.1 ● Key Equity Strategies and Our "Whys"

EQUITY STRATEGIES	RATIONALE (WHAT'S THE PURPOSE?)	IMPORTANCE (WHY DOES IT MATTER?)
Amplify the Talent, Spirit, and Personal Power of MLs	To affirm each ML and recognize their unique assets and strengths	MLs must feel valued, affirmed, seen, heard, and appreciated for who they are and what they can do.
Recalibrate the Curriculum to Accelerate Learning for MLs	To critically examine and revise curricula to include MLs' experiences, worldviews, and cultural perspectives	MLs must have access to culturally, historically, and linguistically responsive, sustaining, integrated curricula that accelerate their academic and linguistic development.
Teach and Assess to Build Student Autonomy, Agency, and Resilience	To ensure that all MLs have access to enriching learning experiences that support their independence and are assessed fairly and equitably	MLs must experience an integrated approach to content, language, literacy, and social-emotional learning and develop agency, autonomy, and resilience.
Harness the Power of Connections and Relationships	To create healthy and safe learning environments and trusting relationships in the classroom, school, and larger communities	MLs must have a strong sense of belonging to thrive as independent and successful learners and members of the community.

CHAPTER ORGANIZATION

While every chapter follows a unique internal organization determined by the topic, there will be some recurring features that offer consistent themes across the topics. Each chapter opens with a sketchnote that infuses the metaphor chosen for the chapter with the chapter content. Claribel González, sketchnote artist and multilingual educator, shares her gift and passion with us as she captures the essence of our message.

At the beginning of each chapter, we will offer a powerful metaphor to draw the reader in. These metaphors not only offer a visual representation and preview of the entire chapter, but also they serve as a powerful tool to make sense of complex ideas. In everyday life, we commonly use metaphors. For example, think of some of the metaphors you used or heard during the pandemic: waves and surges referring to increases in COVID-cases, wartime metaphors such as countries being *under siege* by the virus or *front-line workers* to describe healthcare providers and other essential workers, and so on. How much we all yearned *to see the light at the end of the tunnel*, right? Metaphors empower us and expand the boundaries of thinking beyond some basic processes, so we carefully unpack them and examine their meaning within the context of our current and future reality.

Next, we return to our *why* and establish the urgency for the work depicted in the chapter. The urgency has been there long before the pandemic, yet it was made much more visible by it. We juxtapose the urgency by positioning students' stories and experiences front and center. In the *Student Portraits* section, we present composite vignettes to protect the identities of the students. For some students, we have changed their names, grade levels, and some family characteristics; for others, we combined experiences from multiple contexts, yet we made every effort to preserve the authenticity of the stories. We encourage you to read closely and invite these experiences into your lives. Reflect on them and compare them to your own students' lives. Be inspired to learn about all your MLs' stories. By sharing these stories that are based on or inspired by authentic encounters, we advocate listening to students and talking with them about their interests, realities, needs, gifts, talents, and aspirations.

Following the student portraits, we lay out multiple pathways for approaching equity critically through the lens chosen for the chapter followed by a detailed topic exploration. Each chapter will also invite you to *Look Back and Look Ahead* while staying in the present with ample opportunities for reflection. We have a *Talk to and Listen to Your Students* segment in each chapter that models ways to engage in interactions with your MLs, leaning into those conversations, and learning about your students. We will guide you to ensure that you are fully present and open to hearing what they have to say or what they have to show you in multiple, different modalities of communication and expression.

Throughout the book, you will find several helpful resources and tools to guide you in planning, reflecting on, and implementing equity strategies in your classroom. Under *Equity in Action,* we will share personal accounts, educator and leader reflections, and evidence of successful, authentic examples from classrooms from around the United States related to each chapter topic. Finally, we end each chapter with a call for *Reflections and Actions* as well as offer resources you can use to further explore the topic. Take your time to reflect on the end-of-chapter questions and applications. You may proceed on your own or, whenever feasible, collaboratively tackle these invitations to reflect on and act upon the tasks presented there.

WHY EVERY EDUCATOR SHOULD READ THIS BOOK

This book is for everyone who encounters multilingual learners during their school day. It is for teachers who are at the onset of their career and entered the profession during the pandemic. This book is also for educators who have been in the classroom for many years, yet felt like first year teachers under COVID conditions. Preservice teachers, teacher educators, coaches, and instructional leaders who are grappling with creating the most equitable learning for MLs will also find it useful and relevant. As you each move through the portal to the other side of the pandemic, we hope this book will help you take with you what you need to fully embrace MLs and leave behind what is inequitable, ineffective, and unjust.

Reflections and Actions

1. Earlier in the chapter, we offered our *whys*. Here we are inviting you and your colleagues to consider your own context and define the rationale and capture your *why* for your equity work.

EQUITY STRATEGIES	OWN RATIONALE AND URGENCY FOR EQUITY WORK
Amplify the Talents, Spirits, and Personal Powers of MLs	

EQUITY STRATEGIES	OWN RATIONALE AND URGENCY FOR EQUITY WORK
Recalibrate the Curriculum to Accelerate Learning for MLs	
Teach and Assess to Build Student Autonomy, Agency, and Resilience	
Harness the Power of Connections and Relationships	

2. In this chapter (and the entire book), we suggest treating MLs as *focal students* and by virtue of centering our attention on better understanding them and ensuring an equitable education for them, all students will benefit. What is your argument for or against this claim?

3. Earlier in the chapter, we asked you to briefly reflect on equity practices. Here we ask you to revisit them with your colleagues and establish individual and shared areas of strengths and areas of need. What are the priorities in your context and what are your personal vision and goals for the future?

Assess examples of inequities and their sources in your classroom

Build your capacity to get to know your students

Collaborate and communicate with students, families, and fellow educators

Determine your daily equity moves and actions

Evaluate your impact on students' academic, linguistic, and social-emotional development

Key Resources

Professional Organizations and Research Centers

National Equity Project (A leadership and systems change organization):
https://www.nationalequityproject.org

Learning for Justice (Formerly known as Teaching Tolerance, a project of the Southern Poverty Law Center):
https://www.learningforjustice.org

The Center for Educational Equity (A nonprofit policy and research center at Teachers College, Columbia University):
http://www.centerforeducationalequity.org/

The National Association for Multicultural Education (A nonprofit organization that advances and advocates for equity and social justice through multicultural education):
https://www.nameorg.org/

Professional Books

Hammond, Z. (2015). *Culturally responsive teaching and the brain*. Corwin.

Muhammad, G. (2020). *Cultivating genius: An equity framework for culturally and historically responsive literacy*. Scholastic.

Safir, S., & Dugan, J., with Wilson, C. (2021). *Street data: A next-generation model for equity, pedagogy, and school transformation*. Corwin.

Snyder, S., & Staehr Fenner, D. (2021). *Culturally responsive teaching for multilingual learners: Tools for equity*. Corwin.

Zacarian, D., Calderon, M. E., & Gottlieb, M. (2021). *Beyond crises: Overcoming linguistic and cultural inequities in communities, schools, and classrooms*. Corwin.

CHAPTER 2

Amplify the Talents, Spirits, and Personal Powers of MLS

Look out at a front yard or back yard, a nearby park, the landscape below a terrace, or even your mind's eye and picture a colorful garden. What do you see? Do you imagine a tropical paradise with shiny, lush green leaves and bright flowers? Or do you envision a vegetable garden with ripe zucchini and a bountiful variety of tomatoes hanging from tall vines? Or perhaps you see a fragrant herb garden filled with rosemary, thyme, sage, basil, and dill. Let us consider the garden—whichever kind you imagine—as a metaphor for all our students coming together, a combination of learners with varied talents, passions, and special interests that have the capacity to enrich any classroom.

We are inviting you to our garden, where the flowers bloom during different months, yielding a colorful display throughout the spring, summer, and fall. Just like children, not all the flowers "bloom" at the same time. (Remember the story of *Leo the Late Bloomer* by Robert Kraus and Jose Aruego (1999)?) This garden is filled with such a stunning array of different types of plants, trees, shrubs, and flowers! There are some annuals and perennials growing among green patches of grass, but all are needed to create the diversely beautiful display. Most of all, this garden needs to be tended, nurtured, and sown by those who care for it. To seek the beauty of this parkland, we must recognize and appreciate every plant in it.

Just like our garden with its many unique features, our multilingual learners (MLs) bring their remarkable, varied, and rich cultural and linguistic experiences to our classrooms. But what do we know about caring for them? Do we attend to them in ways that support their academic, linguistic, and social-emotional well-being? To help them grow and blossom, we must recognize how students' cultural backgrounds and personal identities, family histories, generational hopes and dreams for a better life, and their aspirations and personal goals add to the rich, shared experiences in our learning spaces, be it face-to-face, virtual, or any combination of the two. Just as you fully take in the beauty of the garden, let us fully embrace the diversity in our classrooms, schools, and communities and unapologetically advocate for all students to be recognized for their talents, spirits, and personal powers.

THE URGENCY

"Teaching in a post-pandemic world can be overwhelming. But, in this cosmic shift, I am constantly having new experiences where my students teach me and show me how to better support them."

—Nadia Khan-Roopnarine

Recent disruptions to our familiar lives may have taken the greatest emotional toll on our vulnerable school-aged students. Many of our MLs and their families, including second- or third-generation Americans, have also been disproportionately impacted by higher-than-average infection rates and hospitalization cases, more severe socioeconomic losses, and delayed participation in vaccination. On the road to recovery, we must recognize and work toward finding solutions to the many societal ills that were present before the pandemic yet have been drawn even more so into the light because of it—systemic racism, anti-immigrant sentiments and offensive acts, and discrimination against marginalized groups. There is an urgency for us to reflect on and collectively amend the impact of the pandemic on multilingual families but not lose sight of the inner strengths, resilience, and perseverance that our students have gained. Despite the uncertainties, we need to address how to positively respond to the students and their families who have been most impacted by the pandemic and recognize the fact that some communities may continue to feel the effects more acutely for extended periods of time.

We do not know what will come next. Some are convinced life will eventually return to a pre-pandemic state. Others recognize that significant change must occur, are ready to work for it, and welcome a "new normal." We call for action to hold on to what we have learned in these turbulent times. And one of our metaphorical takeaways is to tend to our gardens with affection, devotion, and tenderness! Think of this through the lens of the metaphor with which we opened this chapter: How do we cultivate the growth of our gardens against all odds? What are the sunlight, nutrition, and tender loving care that we can offer to sustain such growth? We are sure that you have seen flowers pushing their way up through clay or a break in the concrete, and you might have wondered how it is even possible for that plant not only to survive but to grow and flourish. Our multilingual students have that power!

Celebrating Our Garden

We recognize the strengths of our high schoolers have who have missed their prom, had their college choices changed because parents lost their jobs, or may not have had a chance to showcase their sports acumen to earn future scholarships but were able to share their graduations on social media with thousands of people!

We take pride in our middle schoolers who are in the midst of finding themselves and stressing over their physical and emotional growth while at the same time noticing that they developed new social and cultural awareness!

We celebrate our elementary students who are beginning to find their identities and learn academic language and applaud that they are still connected with their friends in fun and contactless ways!

We nurture our early childhood youngsters who, a year ago, could not fathom how to use technology and now can interact with schoolmates using the latest technologies and can teach their parents as well!

With thoughtful and intentional classroom-based strategies and by recognizing and affirming our students, we can and will capture and amplify the talents and gifts of our multilingual students.

Our gardens need to blossom and will do so! Let us create a safe, engaging, exciting learning space for all MLs where they can fully embrace their identities, take great pride in their unique cultural and linguistic heritages, and feel proud to share their experiences. All students need to have their voices heard. We have a new opportunity, more than that, a moral obligation to recognize—and show respect for—many of the upheavals that students have experienced as well as the ways they succeeded in overcoming adversity and growing in the midst of crisis.

Pause for a moment and consider your MLs' experiences in the past year or so and reflect on these questions:

- What fears have your students conquered?

- What everyday household chores and more demanding responsibilities have they had?

- How many younger siblings have they tutored or elderly relatives have they taken care of? What positive experiences were found in their caretaking roles?

- How many new apps and technology tools have they tried and mastered?

- What new skills and understandings have they gained that had nothing to do with school?

- On the flip side, what new skills and understandings have they gained that had everything to do with school?

- What barriers did students have to overcome due to hybrid or remote learning?

- How did students develop and maintain relationships with their teachers and other students?

TALK WITH AND LISTEN TO YOUR STUDENTS

How can you gain an understanding of what your students and their families have survived? Begin by listening to them with your full attention and without judgment.

When you speak to your students, lean into the conversations with your whole self. Make sure you are fully attentive and focused as well as open to hearing what they have to say through whatever means they prefer to express themselves. They may share their stories and invite you into their lives through multiple modalities of communication and expression. Many of these modes of communication were introduced during this past year, such as Flipgrid, Padlet, sketchnotes, direct messaging, recordings, iMovies, and more, so let's continue fully using them. For instance, MLs may draw, use visual representations or emojis, or respond in different languages. Communication, through any medium, is what is important. Let's commit to encouraging openness, modeling trust, and recognizing what students have gained during the pandemic and what they will continue to need in a post-pandemic world.

STUDENT PORTRAITS

Eun Woo is a Korean-born student who grew up in the Philippines and then moved to the United States at age 15. He first learned English at an English-medium international school in Manila, having arrived at age six with his brother Choon Woo, who was three years older. At home, the family spoke Korean. On the streets and in the shops, they got along just fine in Tagalog and English. Being so young, Eun Woo's first academic experiences of reading and writing were in English. He found his first few weeks entering school exhausting, but somewhere within the six- to nine-month period, he experienced a "flip of the switch" and began to read and write competently. His confidence with oral language followed. His formative years in the Philippines led to his passion for soccer, his interest in different cultures, and his talent to write poetry.

He left the Philippines with considerable international experience, since many of his friends originally came from around the world. As a high schooler in the United States, his long-term goal has become to go to college and major in government. The pandemic disrupted all his extracurricular activities, but his high school English teacher has left a lasting impression on him. His teacher's strategies included personalized learning and attention to her students' backgrounds. Eun Woo's fascination with English continued to develop as his teacher taught the discipline online via short films, lively Zoom discussions, and interactive Google Slides and Peardecks, by introducing the classics as well as a comprehensive collection of culturally based and contemporary readings. During weekly virtual advisory sessions, this most influential teacher also taught him about bands from around the world, how music was composed, and the literary aspects of lyrics. His favorite band turned out to be Radiohead, as he delved into the musical messages.

Language has remained a passion of Eun Woo's, especially since he needs to be fluent in Korean to speak with his parents and grandparents. He has experienced Korean language loss, as has his brother, after several years in the Philippines, and so in high school they are both taking advanced Korean classes and hope to graduate with the Seal of Biliteracy! He is proud to be able to read novels and newspapers in Korean and communicate better with extended family members.

Eun Woo and his older brother, Choon Woo, also benefited most from meeting friends of different backgrounds and cultures from around the world. Choon Woo's initial experiences of learning to speak, read, and write in English were more difficult, and he attributes that to the fact his brother was younger and at a pre-literate stage when they first moved to the Philippines. He describes himself as shy, and athletics was the way he began to make friends and adjust—first in the Philippines and then in America. For Choon Woo's second move—which was to the United States—the transition was less difficult, and he felt fortunate as he found his well-developed academic routines for studying served him well. Choon Woo became interested in economics based on the passion that one of his teachers shared for the subject. Both young men appreciate the warmth and support they found from their teachers and characterized their multiple moves as stressful but exciting.

Eun Woo's and Choon Woo's stories are unique yet universal in so many ways. Learning about your students' backgrounds, such as Eun Woo and Choon Woo's journey, helps build relationships and a better understanding of how much students have experienced prior to arriving in your classroom and how you may be able to celebrate and better connect students' lived experiences with what you are teaching.

LOOKING BACK, LOOKING AHEAD

How can we challenge the typically negative narrative of "learning loss," as well as the misguided "treatments," such as remediation and/or grade retention? One way to interrupt the learning-loss narrative is with a counternarrative that highlights the successes of our multilingual learners, such as how they were able to learn through synchronous and asynchronous delivery models. Perhaps, most important, we can reframe our current challenges with a positive mindset, deliberate optimism, and an equity lens as we search for the learning gains. There were many positive transformations that took place and are still taking place inside our students' homes, schools, and communities. Here are some "lessons learned" from remote learning that may help showcase the *new* talents and skills multilingual learners developed:

- Many students became comfortable sharing in breakout rooms in ways they might not do when sitting next to each other in a typical classroom.

- Students were able to offer virtual high-fives and emojis to support their peers and demonstrate their spirit, motivation, and devotion to learning.

- Often students helped each other, as well as their teachers, navigate the new instructional technologies.

- Students found ways to navigate the educational system and seek help from teachers, paraprofessionals, and peers.

- Many students were able to chair discussions, as though they were executives at a board meeting.

- Teachers discovered a myriad of ways for students to respond without raising their hands or speaking aloud (red/green images; waterfall responses; the sharing of artifacts from their home; the invitation to parents and community members to be guest speakers).

- Many students exhibited maturity and responsibility that can often come with caring for a younger sibling or grandparent.

- Some MLs served as *language or cultural brokers* for family members as they navigated the health care system and/or social service agencies and became more familiar with community resources and local service providers.

Let us showcase and celebrate the strengths with which students persevered through difficult times. When we know and understand the complex lived experiences of our students through meaningful sharing, we are better positioned to create equitable and safe learning spaces and opportunities. Creating safe and nurturing learning environments for students is certainly not a new concept. What is new, however, are the instances of trauma and loss that many of our students have faced and our call to action to create safe spaces for every child, every day! The safe learning environments will allow places for MLs to succeed and pathways for them to shine. In these spaces, students can feel comfortable developing and sharing their talents and showcasing their personal powers. When MLs feel that they are being seen and heard at school, they will start to share aspects of themselves in ways that will benefit the entire learning community.

How can we best recognize the unique aspects and strengths of our multilingual learners? Take a moment to reflect on the following:

- How can we make sure that equity and social-emotional issues take the forefront in discussions about our students?

- What authentic practices can ensure that our MLs are seen, heard, and noted for what they can do?

- What equitable practices can be implemented that offer multiple ways for students to interact as well as practice their language skills?

- Why will self-care continue to be necessary for students to learn and adopt?

Safir and Dugan (2021) warn educators that they should beware of *superficial equity,* which means adopting equity-centered practices without a clear understanding of the "origins, its purpose, and how to engage in it with depth and authenticity" (p. 39). To foster equitable practices, especially for multilingual learners, we need to have a vision for equitable classrooms.

Take a moment again and reflect on ways your classroom practices can address cultural and social interactions that become more equitable and focus on students' assets, gifts, and persevering spirits.

ESSENTIAL STRATEGIES FOR FOCUSING ON STUDENTS' ASSETS

- Open discussions about how students learned and grew while sheltering in place.

- Review curricula for varied student voice and cultural mirrors.

- Cultivate the talents of multilingual students.

- Elevate students' sociopolitical awareness with an emphasis on how they can leverage their assets toward social justice.

Over a decade ago, Boykin and Noguera (2011) stated it best, "Multiple pathways to success are necessary, and multiple layers of the schooling enterprise must be taken into consideration" (p. 137). It has never been more apt to acknowledge that what MLs need is multiple, meaningful, challenging, and engaging opportunities to learn, opportunities to grow, and opportunities to use their full cognitive, linguistic, and social-emotional repertoires.

AMPLIFY MLS' TALENTS, NURTURE THEIR GIFTS, AND UPLIFT THEIR SPIRITS

Our multilingual learners bring rich, complex cultural and linguistic experiences to our classrooms and schools. Most of us would agree that academic engagement for multilingual learners increases when we design participatory, engaging, and motivating lessons. It is within such lessons that MLs have opportunities to share their backgrounds, gifts, and characterize what drives them to keep going and to be better and more successful learners.

When we talk about developing the personal power of MLs, what do we mean? We are referring to the academic and social journeys that our students must share with their teachers and peers. Rather than keeping such a wide range of vibrant experiences in their back pockets or under wraps, they need to be identified, showcased, and commended. The number of multilingual learners in the United States continues to grow, and this enhanced diversity is an asset. Some of these students are immigrants, and others are children of immigrants or second-, third-, or fourth-generation immigrants, which means we also should learn to appreciate the breadth of familial experiences and cultural diversities of all our multilingual learners. The different background experiences, languages, stories, learning preferences, and histories contribute a special synergy to classrooms and contribute to rich discussions and dynamic curricula. Students have unlimited potentials, and when we say elevate and nurture the personal powers of MLs, we are encouraging all teachers and administrators to bring light to their unique talents and strengths.

Review the following suggestions for enhancing student participation and highlighting assets of multilingual learners. Which of these validate(s) your practice? Which of these challenge(s) your thinking?

- Meet individual student needs through a high-touch, interactive approach.

- Acknowledge how culture can support learning; for instance, embed storytelling, hands-on and inquiry-based assignments in your lessons.

- Assign self-paced homework with choices that students can complete on their own timeline with autonomy to allow for flexibility around outside family responsibilities or work schedules.

- Discuss the content and language targets in your lessons and co-construct ways to meet them.

- Find students from similar backgrounds in other grades (or even across school buildings and districts) to be mentors/mentees and keep the cultural conversations alive.

- Bring realia from home to school and from school to home to share cultural heritages and traditions.

- Encourage writing assignments that delve into background experiences. Students can free-write, pretend they are historians, interview family or community members, or document the historical timelines of families.

- Embrace project-based learning that builds on student curiosity and enhances student agency, with the teacher acting as the guide or facilitator.

- Offer frequent check-ins and formative assessments as targeted, meaningful feedback to students rather than summative exams and traditional grades (narrative feedback and emojis work well, too).

- Reinforce the value of sustaining students' home languages.

Although some would call remote learning a *forced experiment*, others see the positive and often unintended outcomes. We captured some composite voices of MLs that reflect how some students were able to perceive themselves despite the challenges they faced and what they did as learners. Do you recognize any of these students?

"Don't worry teacher, I will help you." (Teacher was having problems with the technology.)

"I feel braver now; I don't rely on my mother as much as she is an essential worker and sleeps in the garage not to make us sick."

"I really enjoy working online and trying out all the new tools. My favorite is Flipgrid."

"I don't feel as much pressure to raise my hand like in class, because I can use an emoji, write in the chat, or simply nod my head."

"My teacher dropped off books in a backpack for me to read and it's like I have my own personal library. I'm reading now more than ever."

"I'm keeping a journal. At first, I only drew a picture of what I did each day so I could show my aunt. But then I started to write and now I fill whole pages about my day and my friends and what I learned."

"I was really upset when I couldn't be in class with my friends, but my teacher let us talk for 5 minutes at the beginning of each lesson. I kinda came out of my shell and now have more friends than ever before."

Tapping into the rich and authentic experiences of our MLs will help them develop and expand their oral and written skills and move them to the next level of language proficiency. We all agree that students do well when they are interested in a topic, share parts of themselves, and authentically engage in the learning process. Creating multiple language and literacy opportunities across all domains (reading, writing, viewing, listening, speaking, and visually representing, WIDA, 2020) daily is a powerful way to affirm our MLs presence in our classrooms and support the next generation of learners.

As you are reading, you probably agree that we need to amplify the talents and better showcase our multilingual learners' unique knowledge. But you might also be asking how this can be done? And at the same time, you might be thinking that our MLs have a cross-section of experiences and different points of access to the English language. We need to create a bridge that leads to equitable practices and is built on a foundation of our MLs' talents, gifts, and passions.

TEN WAYS TO ACCELERATE MLS' LANGUAGE DEVELOPMENT

1. Ask tiered, scaffolded questions. By using probes and questions from a higher level, you challenge your students and ensure that they will move to the next phase of language acquisition quickly. Remember, confidence and spirit will grow as language grows.

2. To enhance learning, specific academic language is needed for students to access the content of lessons. Key vocabulary should be explicitly taught in context and, if possible, prior to a lesson. Model how you learn new vocabulary as an adult and encourage the students to share their best strategies for learning. Make videos with the new vocabulary so MLs can watch them multiple times.

3. Idiomatic expressions should be introduced, discussed, and paired with visual pictures and graphics. Have fun with idiomatic expressions and words with multiple meanings!

4. Have MLs participate in both formal and informal discussions. Use television and educational videos as examples of oral language. Have the students share their favorite YouTube clips and TikToks, if permitted.

5. Ask your MLs about their background knowledge on specific topics and themes and let them be the experts in the class. This will highlight the talents and gifts of students.

6. Although it is important to benchmark students and ensure that teachers who are not prepared with TESOL certification know ML students' level of language development, an overemphasis on the "phase" can hinder learning. For example, knowing when to begin to remove or completely "lose" scaffolds is every bit as important as knowing when to use them. The best approach is to use the levels of language acquisition as a guide and remember that each student is unique, so try to under- rather than overscaffold.

7. MLs should be encouraged to show their mastery through varied products, including drawings, videos, performances, written work, or journals. Can you add to this differentiated list?

8. As a teacher, always model and offer structured activities so the MLs know what to expect and can add their own creativity to assignments.

9. Bring out-of-school linguistic, cultural, and academic experiences into the classroom for acceleration of all students' learning. Bring in guest speakers and local experts and ask them to engage in dialogue with students—an excellent opportunity for students to share their prior knowledge in creative ways.

10. Keep in mind that language is a cross-cutting tool for different disciplines and that students will grow and excel in different subjects and at different momentums. Academic success and individual development should be the focus along the way.

MULTILINGUAL CONSCIOUSNESS: A PATHWAY TO EQUITY

As we work toward the amplification of our MLs' gifts, talents, and spirits, it is helpful to think about language as being the roots in our garden metaphor. Tapping into the students' home languages means that as educators, we are recognizing the students' identity and acknowledging the rich linguistic heritages, languages, and dialects of their home, community, and possibly of the country the students or their families have come from. We call this multilingual consciousness—an intentional, authentic perception that students come to school with a range of linguistic abilities, and these are indeed part of their gifts. The students' language patterns and registers may not reflect that of the teachers or staff, yet this should be viewed as asset-based constructs rather than a manifestation of "sub-standard" English. Think about using the lens of multilingualism and multiliteracy as a benefit and integrating it as part of everyday teaching and learning practices as a call to action. As we invite you to embrace the idea of multilingual consciousness, we can also envision the rich learning opportunities students will have using their full linguistic repertoires as they speak, write, read, and listen in any language available to them and engage in multilingual and multimodal endeavors in and out of class: They create videos, plays, debates, reading logs, illustrated notebooks, inquiry-based projects, and so on across multiple languages and literacies.

EQUITY MOVES TO BOLSTER STUDENTS' TALENTS

Ok, we are mostly vaccinated and back to school. We are out of breath because we have not walked up the school steps in a very, very long time. Some parents have opted to keep their children home, and so the technology is still available for the zoomies and roomies. If the pandemic has taught us anything, it is that as a society, we can pivot on a moment's notice, seek solutions to rising problems, embrace new ideas, be flexible, and change as needed. Educators were at the forefront of doing so! As we enter the next phase of education, we need to remember that our MLs demonstrated resilience and courage and these are the dispositions that will help us to march toward equity in our classrooms and beyond. This next section will focus on ways to develop more equitable practices and unpack ideas on how to engage others in your pursuit of equitable practices.

EMBRACE THE FOLLOWING EQUITY MOVES— THESE STRATEGIES WILL HELP YOU INSPIRE YOUR STUDENTS AND ENCOURAGE YOUR CLASSROOM COMMUNITY TO FOCUS ON EQUITY

1. Assess and reflect on equity in your classroom. Conduct a classroom equity audit looking for equitable systems and "signs" of classroom disproportionality. For instance, are the multilingual students always sitting together? They might choose to do so to feel comfortable in the classroom, but the key question is whether they are being exposed to multiple English language opportunities throughout the day? Are the

MLs benefiting from chances to speak, write, interact, read, and listen (SWIRL) throughout the day within the classroom?

2. Implement carousels at the end of lessons as a means to foster language development. This works well in person or in breakout rooms online. When students have completed their work, they are encouraged to ask questions or offer feedback to their peers. In a live classroom setting, encourage students to walk in one direction and add Post-it notes with positive affirmations. This activity has been lauded as being more interactive and having higher levels of student engagement than the traditional oral presentations at the end of a project.

3. Give students ample processing time. Adopt the idea, *go slow to go fast* as opined by Kimberly Rues (2021). Teachers and their students need time to reacquaint themselves and reconnect. One parent shared with us that her son grew four inches and let his hair grow long during the pandemic. The mother and son worried that the teacher would not recognize her child in person. We all need to take time to build and, in some instances, rebuild and redefine our classroom relationships.

4. Encourage translanguaging, defined by García and Wei (2014) as a process in which, "bilingual speakers select meaning-making features [from multiple languages] and freely combine them to potentialize meaning-making, cognitive engagement, creativity, and criticality" (p. 42). The use of the students' full linguistic repertoires optimizes learning and meaning-making for MLs. In a safe and supportive classroom environment, multiple languages are used regularly and purposefully to build background knowledge and comprehend complex text. Students' home language can be considered a foundation for learning and must be honored as one way to access and build new learning. To support the use of several languages in the classroom, these additional tools may be incorporated into the classroom: anchor charts; multilingual signs, charts, and graphs; electronic devices such as dictionaries or translators; as well as peer bridges who are classmates to offer context, follow-up discussions, or clarifications that support the generation of new knowledge.

5. Start fresh! Create community every day to ensure a sense of belonging for all students whether in person or online. Let's recognize that some students were not able to use cameras consistently during the pandemic and that this did not indicate a lack of interest or unwillingness to learn. Other students simply suffered from Zoom fatigue. Start anew with patience and grace and keep in mind we have all been in a difficult situation.

EMBRACE THE FOLLOWING EQUITY MOVES— THESE STRATEGIES WILL HELP YOU INSPIRE YOUR STUDENTS AND ENCOURAGE YOUR SCHOOL COMMUNITY TO FOCUS ON EQUITY

1. Review student placement. Bring the data together from the classroom audits and look at the different student arrangements across a school. For instance, how are the MLs, gifted students, students with disabilities, and advanced placement students grouped? Do you notice any socioeconomic or racial groups—even if these school arrangements seem unintentional? Safir and Dugan (2021) call this an "equity-focused classroom scan" and suggests that a leadership team use the data to discuss "the current landscape of equity and access" (p. 64).

2. Develop a schoolwide mission of acceleration. Some educators call this philosophy "learning leaps," and others refer to it as positive mindset. Acceleration has traditionally been used when discussing gifted students and the way to challenge them beyond their typical school counterparts. We are using the term to remind teachers that they can strategically choose the curriculum that the students "need to know" to meet age and grade expectations. This may include additional mini-lessons, which are explicitly taught with content and language objectives in mind, or simply offering shorter more fast-paced lessons.

3. Increase cultural opportunities for students within a school to share their backgrounds and personal "funds of knowledge," as introduced over two decades ago by Moll and his colleagues (1992). The hallways in the school can reflect the various social knowledge that is created by highlighting the amazing diversity of backgrounds within one school. This is one way that students, teachers, and the community can establish connections, better understand each other, fight back against cultural prejudice, and enjoy recognizing similarities and embracing differences.

4. Provide culturally and linguistically relevant text for all reading levels. Make sure all students have access to a range of reading resources so that MLs see themselves and their experiences in the curriculum (see Chapter 3 for more).

5. Leverage digital tools. Evaluate accessibility tools that were tested, used, or are needed. All students, not only multilingual learners, should benefit from tools that better help them access the curriculum. Closed captioning, PowerPoints with voiceover, electronic highlighters, screen readers, calculators and low-tech math supports, magnification, and text-to-speech options are all amazing.

6. Integrate students' identities within the curriculum to affirm and acknowledge who they are. Building on their cultural knowledge and affirming their linguistic abilities are critical resources and pathways for higher levels of student engagement (Cummins & Early, 2011).

EMBRACE THE FOLLOWING EQUITY MOVES—THESE STRATEGIES WILL HELP YOU INSPIRE YOUR STUDENTS AND ENCOURAGE YOUR ENTIRE DISTRICT TO FOCUS ON EQUITY

1. Have conversations with school constituents, including teachers, administrators, parents, select students, school boards, and members of the community. Share the perspective that as a collective group, the district must not focus only on what was lost during the pandemic but rather focus on what was gained from the pandemic experience and how to sustain it.

2. Create a district improvement plan or strategic plan. Address all critical issues of what school life may entail on the other side. Establish key focus areas and be sure ML perspectives and needs are included in the solutions.

3. Form action groups to conduct needs assessments. What resources will need to be garnered for students who may have not "logged on" or "checked-in" at all? Decisions about attendance may need to be made as students are reengaged in schooling. Is there a way to support parents and families who have lost their jobs or suffered reduced salaries? Swap shops, food banks, and after-school programs may be examples of community endeavors that need to be continued in the next few years.

4. Keep up with technology integration, provide ongoing training for teachers, and ensure equitable access to devices for all. Discussions about the successes of technology need to take place, so districts can decode the traditional assumptions about how children learn. Many students showed an increased aptitude for learning online and districts can re-think how schooling is delivered. For instance, in overcrowded districts, we now know that some students will opt for simultaneous or concurrent learning. We can consider whether snow days in colder states are even needed anymore if students and teachers can work from home. Most important, we need to quantify the cost of computers, Wi-Fi, and software. This is a unique time to collect data on the technological side of instructional delivery. Districts can consider building infrastructures that will sustain schools and schooling in the future.

5. Survey students and their parents or conduct student- and parent-focus group sessions arranged by language communities. Ask questions about what worked, learning preferences, and perhaps even about barriers to learning. This is one way to include the community and use the findings to design intentional strategies for student and parent engagement in the future. Many parents have reported that they have a new understanding of the curriculum and new insight into what their children experience daily. Now is the time to tap into the feelings, experiences, hopes, and dreams that families have for their children's future.

Multilingual learners must be loved, cared for, and appreciated for who they are and what they can do! They need acknowledgments and affirmations! They require safe learning environments, unconditional support and encouragement, and warmth from the educators who have the privilege to work with them.

BRIDGES TO EQUITABLE PRACTICES: INFUSING THE SPIRIT OF LEARNING

Have you read any of the many recent reports that brought larger, societal inequities to light? Have you heard anecdotal accounts offered by teachers, students, or parents of multilingual learners feeling marginalized and excluded when working from home due to lack of resources, access to technology, and so on? Let's commit to providing equitable access to external resources while also nurturing the internal resources MLs, their families, and communities have built. Try these research-based suggestions for continued support for increasing capacity for multilingual learners:

Embrace biculturalism and multilingualism: Many students are biracial and bicultural, which means that they successfully function in different cultures that may possess different values, mores, traditions, beliefs, and even behaviors. Let's consider how we might change our expectations so students' bilingualism may be fully recognized as an asset. For example, allow processing time in students' home languages, invite them to share cultural artifacts that are important to them, and create learning environments that celebrate students' individual identities.

Teach cultural pluralism: Create an atmosphere and learning environment in the classroom that models acceptance, understanding, and the positive relationships that come about when people from varied cultures interact. Let's emphasize that no one's culture or background should ever be viewed as inferior or superior. This is a thoughtful process that will take time to internalize.

Reject bias: No matter the grade or age level of your students, challenge any speech that is prejudicial or degrading. When biased language is used, work with the students to explore the origin, offensiveness, or exclusionary foundation and consider replacement language that is supportive and affirming.

Recognize fatigue: This past year we heard the terms mask fatigue and Zoom fatigue. These are a real aspect of overload, and teachers and administrators must recognize it and make space for it. One way is to include brain breaks both in person and online.

Teach financial literacy: Students need to understand the financial and economic inequalities that were exposed during the pandemic. This is not just learning about everyday money transactions but deeper issues that often affect minorities, such as student debt and budgeting.

Respectfully challenge: In many classrooms, the conversations are polite, and students are encouraged to be kind to each other. Yet we cannot be silent in the face of aggression or violence against any individual or groups of students. Students must learn how to respectfully share their opinions and learn to acknowledge—even if they do not agree—the positions of others. They must also learn how to stand up against prejudice and discrimination, challenge offensive or oppressive words and actions, and advocate for themselves and others to be treated fairly and equitably.

EQUITY IN ACTION

Andrea Dell'Olio, ENL teacher at the High School for Health Professions & Human Services, New York City, shared with us her personal journey to equity:

At my first job as an ENL teacher at a school in East Harlem, I immediately recognized the brilliance in all my students—those who were technically classified as English language learners, as well as the other diverse learners who were added to my classes for "intervention" due to lack of school resources. I sometimes wondered how I could view my students so differently from other teachers at the school. Every day I had the privilege of teaching and learning from kindergarten through fourth-grade students who could ask insightful, thought-provoking questions about the world, build robots from scratch, and not only identify but create poems interspersed with figurative language, among many other impressive skills and talents. "But he's still a Level B," classroom teachers would complain, referring to a student's reading level, which was several letters behind what the reading program deemed appropriate. "He's just not on grade level," they would proclaim sadly, as if it were a life sentence. It was during those early years of teaching that I finally began to understand that the perspective we have, of our students and of learning, is vital to creating equitable conditions in our schools and to fostering the love of learning that every student deserves to feel. Now, that very perspective has enabled me to guide my ninth-grade English language learners to proficiently read Chaucer and relate it to their own lives, produce high-level "essay-worthy" questions that are on par with the ones teachers might create, engage in Socratic seminars to discuss the topic of educational injustice faced by immigrant and migrant students in the

United States, and write convincing argumentative essays on the value of Ethnic Studies in schools. When we truly believe our students can do anything, they will always exceed our expectations.

Over the years, I have often felt like every day there was a new impediment to the success of my students. Many times, it was not just a feeling, it was the reality of working in a system designed to uplift some and tear others down. Whether it is forcing students to take standardized tests during a global pandemic, having them repeat a grade because they did not complete enough homework that year, or relegating them to the back of a classroom to color because "they don't speak English," the frustration increases but so does my drive to help eradicate these unjust practices. I am reminded to continually question how we define learning, literacy, and education, and how to celebrate the limitless gifts of our students. I am inspired to teach in a way that centers, celebrates, and highlights the gifts of all learners. Throughout my teaching career, one thing has remained constant: that students will always be successful when teachers create the conditions and the environment for them to flourish. Though equity in schools cannot fully be attained until all racist systems are completely dismantled and new, anti-racist systems are built, the instructional methods and approaches we utilize can be vehicles for establishing an equitable playing field in the classroom. Hence, as systems are overhauled, changing teachers' perspectives and their approaches to teaching can be a powerful way to move instruction toward a more equitable education world.

I fully believe and have seen firsthand that there is nothing my students cannot do, though my own perspective and philosophy as a teacher have undergone many transformations. I myself have shifted from viewing literacy as limited to reading and writing, to understanding literacy as brilliance or competence in any area. Our students deserve teachers who reject that there are limitations to their brilliance and who understand student learning is vastly different from test scores, reading levels, and outdated curricula. Teachers, most of whom just want to see their students succeed, sometimes just need that one shift in their mindset to open their eyes to a new world of student learning and possibility. My ultimate goal is to guide teachers to embody these high expectations, a progressive vision, the bold and effective instructional methods touted by experts and advocates of the diverse learning community, and a perspective that sees the true brilliance and many levels of literacy that all students bring to their classroom.

PARTING THOUGHTS

We now know there is not only one pathway to learn. To be successful, our multilingual learners need support from all constituencies in schools as well as from their parents and communities. Teachers must find ways to accelerate learning and amplify the successes of MLs. We can work to build safe spaces for honest conversations, places that nurture individual and collective spirit, and encourage us to share multiple perspectives with our diverse students. The march toward equity requires intentional, actionable practices that permeate classrooms with accountable routines while amplifying the talents and passions of our multilingual learners. In the process of reflection over the last year, it has become even clearer that our MLs must feel valued and affirmed as well as appreciated for who they are. Most importantly, educators need to support MLs so that they are comfortable sharing their big ideas and passions, their hobbies and interests, their backgrounds and personal experiences, their cultures and languages, their gifts and talents, and of course, their hopes and dreams.

Reflections and Actions

1. We compared the diversity among students to the beautiful variety of flowers and plants in a garden. In what ways has this metaphor supported your understanding of the complex experiences of our MLs? What other ways can you capture the rich diversity among MLs?

2. Early in this chapter, we introduced two multilingual learners and encouraged you to develop a deeper understanding of all your MLs. What approaches have you used to get to know your students?

3. We have advocated for creating a safe, engaging, exciting learning space for MLs. In what ways does this approach help them fully embrace their identities? How does it make them feel in your classroom?

4. How can students share their successes and spirit for learning with their peers, teachers, and parents?

Key Resources

· ·

Centre for Educational Research on Languages and Literacies (CERLL):

https://www.oise.utoronto.ca/cerll/

The 2020 edition of WIDA Standards:

https://wida.wisc.edu/teach/standards/eld

To further explore multiliteracies:

https://newlearningonline.com/multiliteracies

CHAPTER 3

Recalibrate the Curriculum to Accelerate Learning for Multilingual Learners

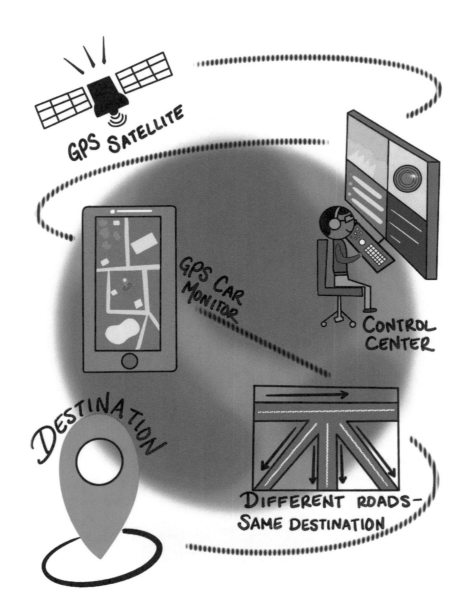

*T*he curriculum is a global positioning system (GPS). It provides users with information to navigate the concepts, subject matter, learning goals, instructional delivery methods, and assessment practices within a given course of study. Its organization provides educators with guidance about which roadways to take to facilitate student-learning experiences. Similar to the milestones or signposts a GPS provides its travelers, the curriculum furnishes learning targets and formative and summative assessments for teachers to determine whether or not students are on the right track.

The same way a GPS supports drivers with information to arrive at their destinations with accuracy and ease, the curriculum should support teachers by including cutting-edge, research-informed best practices for content knowledge delivery. And when providing instruction for multilingual learners (MLs), the curriculum should also map out how language learning can be integrated with content instruction similar to the way smart highway systems are now being built to integrate their technology with our mobile devices.

We also must recognize that a GPS may not always be accurate. In spite of careful adherence to GPS directions and its declaration that "you have arrived at your destination," many of us have felt bewildered when we have been led to the edge of a dead-end street or have entered a construction zone with multiple detours ahead. The feeling one gets from hitting a dead end is very similar to the way many of us felt when the pandemic drove us out of our classrooms and into remote learning environments. Overnight, our curricula were upended, as was our very relationship with teaching! During this time, the curriculum as it stood no longer provided the needed direction, and many of us felt the system in place was no longer offering the much-needed guidance.

One of the most important aspects of a GPS is that it requires human input—users need to engage with the system for it to work. Without such input, a GPS cannot offer any viable information or support for getting to the appropriate destination. Furthermore, it frequently allows travelers a choice of which set of directions to take to arrive at a chosen destination. In the same way, the curriculum needs to be accessible, functional, and flexible and provide the needed guidance to teachers to develop multiple access points for instruction. For this to occur, we need to continually be engaged with its contents and fully understand its context to judge whether or not what is being taught is worth knowing and also making a positive and equitable impact on students as well as connections to their lived experiences.

The GPS is a game-changing invention, but we still need to be aware of our surroundings or we'll end up in the wrong place. In the same way, a curriculum, as written, can appear to be groundbreaking, but if it is not serving our students and getting them where they need to go—how do we know? We need to fully understand the context of our classroom and know our students before the curriculum is accessible and effective for all.

We know that a GPS is much improved when the system is updated; when this occurs, it can not only provide clearer navigation but also alert travelers to important services, food, lodging, and points of interest to make a trip run smoothly. In the same way, the curriculum needs to be renewed and refreshed to consider its many dimensions and supports for teachers and students and continually redeveloped to be a *part of an interactive system for learning that is frequently re-examined, refined, and recalibrated.*

THE URGENCY

"Like many others, our school is starting to really reckon with decolonizing the curriculum and aligning assessment and instruction with what students can do, instead of what they don't know yet."

—Meghan Lydon

As we collectively ponder the urgency to recalibrate the curriculum, a critical question comes to mind—*What is worth teaching and knowing, and who is making the decisions about what we teach?* The pandemic to a large extent gave us license to question the status quo; in fact, it compelled us to do so as we began to closely examine scope and sequence guides and curriculum maps and shifted our instructional practices to meet the demands of remote learning for our students. Consequently, it became more apparent that the standardized curriculum we teach suffers from the outdated notion that it serves *all* students. In many ways, we have been taught several lessons on that score. Even though we were aware of the low-expectation or nonexistent curricula in place for many of our MLs before schools began to close, teaching classes virtually or, later on, in hybrid settings made us even more mindful of how the needs of MLs are not served by our standard sets of curricula! The urgency became more apparent than before—we need to take action to remedy the situation to create equitable learning environments for all students.

When we invited teachers to respond to questions about their experiences with recalibrating the curriculum due to COVID-19, many of their answers centered on how they navigated and implemented the current curriculum during the pandemic, prioritized standards, and reduced content, or they described changes that occurred in their instructional delivery and collaborative practices. Some teachers responded that there were no changes at all that occurred. However, one particular response caught our attention. It described how the pandemic was the impetus for teacher agency and action to consider and incorporate student needs and align them with the curriculum. This teacher's response also related how the pandemic became an incentive for teachers to choose which and how units of study were implemented. In short, is it possible to claim that the pandemic spawned a new generation of thoughtful and reflective practitioners? Has it perhaps changed the way we look at our jobs, with educators driving the curriculum instead of the other way around?

As we anticipate teaching MLs in the post-pandemic era, what shifts in curriculum development are essential as we return to brick-and-mortar classrooms? When we closely examine curriculum and instruction for the sake of MLs through an equity lens, what comes to light is how they are routinely placed in classes that offer simplified content and texts, tasks that focus on isolated language skills, classrooms ill equipped with up-to-date technology, and often no viable curriculum that offers MLs access to the grade-level content. Therefore, moving forward, we advocate for curricula that fully integrate content and language instruction for the sake of MLs and assures equitable learning opportunities.

As part of aligning curricula to create equitable learning opportunities for MLs, we must ask *who* is making decisions about the subject matter being taught. In order to recalibrate the curriculum, we must pay careful attention to what we are teaching as much as we focus on how instruction is being delivered. For this reason, developing and implementing curricula that intentionally and meaningfully integrate the history and culture of all students is essential to providing a diverse and equitable education that fosters MLs' academic success.

The curriculum should not only specify content and learning benchmarks but also guide teachers on how students learn best by using equitable assessment practices. Consider how a student-centered curriculum might provide opportunities for self-directed learning, an increased responsibility on the part of students to identify their own instructional needs, a collaborative process for defining or redefining expectations for success, the freedom for students to choose resources based on personal connections, passions, or interests, and active engagement in individual and collaborative inquiry that supports the development of and opportunities for language and literacy practice and social-emotional growth.

All in all, the curriculum must provide multiple pathways to the same destination. In light of the pandemic, we firmly reject the notion of the frequently cited learning loss and instead, argue for replacing remediation and deficit-thinking with acceleration and for students and teachers to co-create authentic curricula that are relevant, rigorous, and reflect the lived experiences of all of our students.

STUDENT PORTRAITS

Yazhini and Ayesha, 16-year-old twin sisters, have attended a suburban high school on the outskirts of a major U.S. city since the September before the COVID-19 outbreak began. Living together with their large extended family, originally from India, they were hard hit by the pandemic—losing their grandmother at its onset. Their father and mother also became ill but made a fairly quick recovery. The family suffered a short time from food insufficiency when both parents were unable to work, and they relied on their local temple's food bank for basic essentials. Everyone in their household continues to worry about family members and friends who remain in India as the news reports the rapid escalation of COVID infections there.

Before the pandemic hit, the twins spent a great part of their school day in a multi-grade English language development (ELD) class with other MLs who ranged in age from 14 to 19. The ELD class instruction focused primarily on students' learning English grammar, basic vocabulary, and speaking and listening skills. There was no set curriculum for the class, and no grade-level content was addressed in any systematic way—much of the materials gathered by their well-intentioned ELD specialist who made every effort to use high-low books (high interest-low readability) that the district purchased and touted for MLs. However, at the height of the pandemic, all schools in their district switched to remote learning. This shift in instructional delivery proved to be challenging at first for Yazhini and Ayesha. Their family did not own laptops or tablets or reliable Internet, and while they waited for the school to provide the needed technology, they borrowed their parents' phones for remote lessons.

When the new academic year began the following fall, their school switched to hybrid learning, in which students rotated between in-person and online classes. This new schedule became a wonderful opportunity for the twins. Due to the allocation of resources and the need to use school space efficiently, students attended in-person school days according to their grade level. Yazhini and Ayesha now found themselves in grade-level classes with their English-fluent peers. In these classes, they received support from either their ELD teacher or an instructional aide. Everyone soon discovered that with adequate scaffolding, lesson pacing, and translanguaging, Yazhini and Ayesha were capable of meeting the challenges of the more rigorous general education curricula. When in-person school finally returns full time next fall, the twins are hoping that they will be able to remain in regular content-area classes.

Let's stop and critically reflect on Yazhini and Ayesha's experiences in light of recalibrating the curriculum to accelerate learning for MLs.

Consider their encounter with the more rigorous curriculum of grade-level classes when they began hybrid learning and ponder these questions:

- How did Yazhini and Ayesha react to being in grade-level classes? How might their responses challenge traditional beliefs about the abilities of MLs?

- What supports in the grade-level classes were critical to Yazhini and Ayesha's success? What additional teaching practices might support MLs to have access to more rigorous curricula?

- Consider how educators' beliefs about "appropriate" curricula for MLs might affect student performance. Have you had any experiences with students exceeding expectations to perform academically with rigorous content? If so, what supports were necessary for this to occur?

- How might students develop ownership of the curriculum when their agency and curiosity are nurtured?

- How might you advocate for all teachers to use an equity lens and closely examine their curricula? Is it deliberately inclusive of multiple perspectives and rich, diverse instructional materials? Does it allow for multiple ways of knowing, learning, and demonstrating new understandings and skills?

- How might your advocacy further the creation of high-achieving class cultures that support the use of rigorous curricula for all students?

LOOKING BACK, LOOKING AHEAD

Over the past several decades, teaching MLs has involved many shifts in practice from changes in curriculum, teaching approaches, and overall beliefs about their capabilities to learn academically, to develop linguistically, and to engage in the overall school community. These shifts have influenced the many programs, resources, and texts that have been developed and implemented for their instruction. Looking back before the turn of this century, school-age MLs who spoke little or no English were frequently placed in segregated ELD programs that focused on developing the four language domains—listening, speaking, reading, and writing—in that order. The curriculum largely targeted nonacademic topics, such as the family, the neighborhood, food and drink, transportation, and so on; we know now that these programs did not adequately prepare MLs to accomplish grade-level schoolwork. From the mid-1980s–2000, ELD instruction began to shift, with the onset of instructional models that fostered the development of English language and literacy skills while providing students with opportunities to learn grade-appropriate content (Chamot & O'Malley, 1986; Echevarria et al., 2000). Yet for the most part, MLs continued to be segregated from general education classes and their fluent-English peers, and they remained in ELD programs whose curricular subjects, texts, and materials offered predominately white, Euro-centric perspectives that did not reflect their lived experiences. Although there has been more focus on incorporating diverse voices, in the form of lesson topics, literature selections, and cultural perspectives into the curriculum, these attempts have often missed the mark. Typical attempts at providing students with varied viewpoints have resulted in a segregated, token representation of Black and Brown people through add-on curricula that celebrate *heroes* and *holidays*, such as heritage months, and position the histories of non-dominant cultural groups outside of the standard or scripted curricula.

In more recent years, there have been much needed, greater strides to integrate content and language instruction for MLs who are English learners. These classes gave rise to team teaching or co-teaching in which one teacher is certified in content-area instruction and the other an ELD specialist or having a dually certified teacher to instruct MLs in both content and language. Yet in these classes, the content curriculum continues to dominate instruction, with ELD used to support the learning of subject matter. Interestingly enough, although instructional models have shifted, the curriculum frequently has not.

Before you look ahead with us, stop and critically reflect on the curriculum you presently use to guide you to develop lessons for MLs. Do you:

- Rely on prepackaged or digital curricula for stand-alone ELD classes?

- Focus on nonacademic subject matter to develop basic communicative English language skills?

- Depend on whatever content curriculum the classroom teacher is using?

- Adapt the general education curricula for your students when a class is co-taught?

- Reinforce the same topics being taught in general education curricula when MLs are pulled out of their regular classes for ELD instruction?

- Scaffold general education curricula for MLs and differentiate instruction for students' various language proficiency levels in co-taught and/or stand-alone classes?

- Have no set ELD curriculum and have to create your own?

- Turn to state standards, grade-level content, and student assessment data to guide you to develop an ELD curriculum?

- Wish for some guidance in the form of a curriculum map or scope and sequence or something more tangible that would support your instruction with MLs?

As we look toward the future, we need to reimagine the curriculum for MLs by being ever mindful of how classroom spaces serve to shape students' identities. For this reason, the curriculum being constructed for those spaces must also reflect the lives of the students who occupy them as well as open students to new perspectives. If we apply Bishop's (1990) metaphor from Chapter 1 about how books offer readers windows, sliding glass doors, and mirrors into the human experience, we can look ahead to accelerate the curriculum for MLs so that

- its windows offer students multiple perspectives about subject matter,

- its sliding glass doors invite students to walk through and experience diverse viewpoints through the eyes of others' feelings, motivations, and intentions, and

- its mirrors reflect and affirm their unique backgrounds, customs, beliefs, cultures, and personal experiences.

As we recalibrate the curriculum for MLs, we use an equity lens to determine whether or not it represents a blend of cultural voices that paint an inclusive vision of the values, mindsets, language traditions, and norms that make up our pluralistic American society and beyond as well as forge more equitable pathways for MLs to meet with school success by rethinking the curriculum.

RECALIBRATING THE CURRICULUM

When considering how to reshape the curriculum for the sake of MLs, we focus on ways in which we can purposefully lift up traditionally marginalized voices, strengthen the integration of rigorous language and content teaching and equitable assessment practices, and represent multiple perspectives so students see their lives reflected in the curriculum as well as the lives of others. Of equal importance, we must advocate for dismantling inequities in opportunity by repositioning the common narratives of the dominant culture, decolonizing the curriculum so that it incorporates multiple points of view honoring the histories and experiences of previously marginalized, minoritized, or overlooked communities, and razing the misguided assumptions some educators maintain about the abilities and future potentials of MLs.

When working with students who are acquiring fluency in English, Bunch and Walqui (2019) advise us to shift away from simplifying curricular content and intensify, amplify, enhance, elaborate, extend, and expand our students' knowledge and understandings of language and content. They further argue that "classroom teachers are the most important curriculum developers, both in terms of creating their own materials and adapting those created by others" (p. 3). Yet, simplification of language and content remains a common recommendation given to teachers of students learning English, to say nothing of how most teachers feel their hands are tied when it comes to tailoring curricula for the sake of MLs. This notion of simplified instruction in the form of a watered-down curriculum only serves to remove students from grade-level subject matter and subsequently increases the gap in educational opportunities and achievement. All things considered, we educators must collaborate to take on the challenge to develop curricula for MLs that will lead to their academic success.

To recalibrate the curriculum, we explore five key ideas for focusing efforts to re-examine and reshape the guidance provided for all teachers of MLs as follows:

- Curricular content—*what* we (plan to) teach

- Curricular lesson delivery—*how* we teach

- Integration of content, language, literacy, and social-emotional learning in the written curriculum (see Chapter 4 for more)

- Equitable, multidimensional assessment measures that shape the curriculum delivery

- Teacher and student advocacy for equity

Before we begin to explore ideas for transforming curricula for MLs, we would like to offer you a reminder—none of this work can be accomplished by a single person. Yet there only needs to be one person to get it started.

CURRICULAR CONTENT: WHAT WE TEACH

The reasons for curricular change may be simple, but the task is quite complex, and incorporating inclusive content is not an easy undertaking. So you might be thinking, *where do I begin?* We all know that the curriculum should be devised and revised by teachers, but the reality is that many of us are handed a curriculum to follow, and pressures from school administrators and state policies often dictate what should and shouldn't be taught. So the question to ask might be *where can I begin?*

Start by examining the current unit you are teaching or a unit you most recently taught to determine the following:

- Are students' curiosity, passion, and excitement for learning incorporated?

- Do students shape the curriculum through learner-centered, inquiry-based authentic explorations?

- Are the perspectives of non-dominant cultures represented?

- Are multiple perspectives addressed for all subject matter?

- Are the authors of print and digital readings and resources diverse in race, gender, and ethnicity?

- Are diverse cultural heritages, histories, and intersecting identities reflected in readings and resources?

- Does the unit content support critical discussion for students to develop multiple understandings and challenge stereotypes?

- Does the unit serve to elevate people of color or those with historically marginalized identities?

- Are the knowledge and real-life experiences of your students reflected?

- Does the unit provide real-world connections?

- Does the unit incorporate student learning with current environmental, health, social-emotional, or political concerns?

- Does the unit provide students with opportunities to critically reflect on the worldview of others as well as their own?

By examining the curriculum, we can ensure that curricular barriers to achievement are lifted with the promotion of culturally responsive instruction that incorporates and values the culture, languages, and perspectives of people whose voices have traditionally been neglected. Yet we must also note that the nature of culture is dynamic, and a commitment to curricular revision is a continuous pursuit. So as you consider what to teach, *what do you retain, what do you remove, what do you add, and what do you revise? And how can you best serve the needs of culturally and linguistically diverse students within the framework of local and state standards?* The following are a set of guidelines for considering what to include in the curriculum:

- Make students partners in creating curriculum, materials, and assignments that are relevant to them.

- Develop and maintain subject matter that is rigorous, grade appropriate, and culturally responsive to ensure students are cognitively engaged.

- Identify the prerequisite knowledge and skills needed for success and map out how attention can be paid to students who need to build them; create opportunities for accelerated learning through multimodal activities (see chapter 4 for more).

- Focus on what is essential to students' enduring understandings of the world that have lasting value beyond the classroom and connect with their lived experiences.

- For each unit of study, uncover subject matter by carefully crafting critical questions according to Bloom's taxonomy to ensure high levels of thinking, and create ample opportunities for student-driven inquiry.

- Develop your knowledge base so that your curriculum can stretch beyond the inclusion of token contributions of marginalized groups.

CURRICULAR LESSON DELIVERY: HOW WE TEACH

When recalibrating the curriculum, we must discover how to shift away from traditional notions of covering the curriculum as it is written—having a predetermined set of subject topics, providing rote and passive learning tasks, implementing standardized assessments as the sole driver of instruction, and highly regarding the content more than the process of developing language and knowledge application and synthesis. We must also consider how to deliver instruction for MLs—by recognizing and affirming the various strengths and abilities of this diverse and heterogeneous group of students and approaching instruction in ways that provide all students not just access to, but also active engagement with the core curriculum. Although there are no simple approaches to teaching MLs, we focus on five overarching practices for successful learning that should be a part of every lesson: (a) teacher clarity, (b) activating prior knowledge and building background, (c) academic language and literacy, (d) critical thinking, and (e) student collaboration.

Teacher clarity (Fisher et al., 2017). To make lessons comprehensible, teachers routinely set and share with students the purpose for instruction, align benchmarks as success criteria, and clearly link tasks and assignments to learning targets and assessment outcomes. During direct instruction, teachers offer clear explanations that include modeling, demonstrations, visuals, realia, multimedia presentations, and multiple means of making information understandable. Teacher clarity also involves supporting students through guided practice before they are asked to work independently.

Activating prior knowledge and building background. Understanding the context for learning is critical for students to be able to grasp and retain new information. At the onset of a lesson, teachers use instructional time wisely by using various strategies to engage students to recall information and drawing from their own personal experiences that will serve as the basis for the lesson. If students do not have the required background knowledge, teachers must create opportunities for students to build that needed information to access new subject content.

Academic language and literacy integration. All teachers must support students to develop language and literacy practices for their success in core curricular subjects. Students need ample opportunities to practice using language and engage in continuous critical dialogue, write in various genres, interact with teachers and their peers, read and analyze grade-level texts, and actively listen and critically respond to information. Through direct instruction, careful attention must also be paid to key words and phrases as well as how those words are strung together to create sentences and larger pieces of text. Students can only develop competence in content-area subjects by strengthening their understanding and use of language and developing their social-emotional learning.

Critical thinking. Questioning is an essential element to stimulate student thinking. Yet, novice and veteran teachers alike often do not spend sufficient time strategically developing questions that challenge students to think critically and remain cognitively engaged. We need to shift away from asking students questions off the top of our heads—the questions that focus on checking student recall of basic facts—and switch to open-ended questions that draw students in to think more deeply about the whys, hows, and what-ifs of the subject matter. We must also build student autonomy by creating opportunities for student-led discussions, in which they develop their own critical questions. Inquiry-based and problem-based learning are additional ways to activate students' interest, curiosity, and engagement while they explore particular topics and problem-solve to find answers to the teacher's and their own questions.

Student collaboration. MLs who need to develop their English language fluency as well as all students benefit from collaborative activities in which classmates work in pairs or teams to complete assignments in which they explain content, make predictions, apply information to problem solve, compare ideas, critique a third party's work, and so on. In turn, these group tasks foster oral communication and higher-order thinking, increase student autonomy and agency, and allow students the time and opportunity to negotiate diverse ideas and opinions as well as develop social-emotional skills. Tasks may be open-ended, supporting student independence and authentic interactions, or scaffolded through the use of sentence stems so that students can practice the use of specific language forms to communicate with one another in meaningful ways.

INTEGRATION OF CONTENT AND LANGUAGE LEARNING IN THE WRITTEN CURRICULUM

All teachers of MLs should strive to provide rigorous, grade-level academic content that is aligned with appropriate English language development goals. To create an effective curriculum for teaching MLs, language and content instruction must be integrated with specific guidance on how to scaffold instruction for students to develop their language and literacy practices and content knowledge in tandem. The written curriculum should also provide an array of ideas for comprehensible learning opportunities that support the balanced development of the four language domains— speaking, writing, reading, and listening. We advocate for a curriculum for MLs that seriously and explicitly integrates language development with content learning, equitably targeting and assessing each of these instructional components so that all students thrive. We believe the guidance that *all* teachers need should not be placed in supplemental documents to the general education curriculum to support the learning of MLs; instead, we promote placing specific academic language and literacy development opportunities for MLs directly into any written curriculum to ensure all teachers are supported in this endeavor so that:

- All MLs have equal access to and instruction from content-area experts

- All MLs have equitable opportunities to be taught the same curriculum as their grade-level peers

- All educators are prepared to teach MLs

- All educators take up the challenge of how to address the basic or foundational, intermediate, and discipline-specific language and literacy needs of MLs

- All educators know how to create opportunities for language learning along with the development of content-area knowledge and skills

EQUITABLE, MULTIDIMENSIONAL ASSESSMENT MEASURES THAT SHAPE THE CURRICULUM

One of the most important aspects of promoting educational equity for MLs is the identification of assessment practices that yield accurate accounts of student learning. Understanding the need for assessment strategies to determine student outcomes and represent the comprehensive abilities of the whole child is a critical goal. For this reason, we advocate for collaboratively devised assessments, including authentic performance assessments to gauge students' understanding and application of both content and language and document the growth of MLs over time. To support the process of capturing accurate assessment data for MLs, we propose the following:

- Shift away from limiting curricula that only support the teaching of subject matter that is tested on high-stakes exams.

- Eliminate overreliance on the often inaccurate data compiled from standardized tests to make decisions about how MLs are placed in classes and special programs.

- Focus on gathering data from assessments that give students fair and equitable opportunities to demonstrate their learning.

- Rely more on data obtained from authentic, teacher-designed performance assessments that indicate student progress in content, language, and literacy development.

- Use rubrics to assess students' oral and written responses, hands-on projects, and experiments, and to offer students feedback.

- Invite students to compile portfolios of their work and collaboratively gauge their progress over time.

- Provide students with opportunities for self-assessment, peer-assessment, and assessing their and others' performance in group assignments.

TEACHER AND STUDENT ADVOCACY FOR EQUITY

To promote equity, we must feel sufficiently empowered to unapologetically raise our voices and advocate for MLs. Although it is vital for school leadership to be committed to equity work, we can no longer leave the impetus for this work in their hands alone. Therefore, teacher, as well as student self-advocacy, are critical to sustaining the work of curricular revisions that are long overdue. As educators, we witness daily the effects of poor education policies and practices and ultimately their consequences for MLs. We can no longer stand idly by while decisions for students are being made without us or student input. Similarly, equity work in curriculum and instruction must also include students' voices, passions, and talents. Their agency, autonomy, and resilience are critical resources that must be tapped and appreciated (see Chapter 4 for more).

What can we do to make our voices heard? Smith and colleagues (2017) identify the basics for building equitable learning opportunities as follows: "Any school taking the bold and necessary steps to open up opportunities to learn for all students must be prepared to allocate new resources or reallocate existing resources" (p. 90). The problem most teachers face is that they do not have the power or influence to determine where funds are allocated. However, they do have the capacity and agency to act purposefully, advocate for the needs of their students, promote self-advocacy among students, and contribute to the improved awareness and understanding of equity issues with their colleagues. We must actively advocate for the curricular recalibration that will lead to the success of our multilingual learners as follows:

- Foster a shared vision of change and promote collaborative grassroots efforts with other teachers to shape the curriculum for the sake of MLs.

- Encourage colleagues to engage together in professional learning through book studies, virtual and in-person workshops, professional organization conferences, and so on, to identify and address how to better align curriculum to the histories and experiences that reflect the diversity of MLs.

- Recognize and affirm the real-world experiences of the MLs and help create ways for sharing new and enhanced curricula within the school and larger community.

- Urge leadership to conduct an equity audit of the curriculum.

- Promote the inclusion of teacher-initiated curriculum revisions for the sake of MLs.

- Challenge the system to ensure all students have equitable access to course offerings and extracurricular activities.

TALK WITH AND LISTEN TO YOUR STUDENTS

In the brief yet startling essay, *I Taught Them All*, about the nature of the curriculum and its impact on children's lives, Naomi White (1944) seriously considered how her instruction transformed the students in her charge over the span of ten years, much of which occurred during the Great Depression. Living and teaching during such unprecedented times, Ms. White, a high school English teacher from Muskogee, Oklahoma, describes some of her former pupils, how they were as children when they first were seated in her classes, and what they became later in their lives. As she muses over the current plight of each one of them, the author ends the essay as follows:

> All of these pupils once sat in my room, sat and looked at me gravely
> across worn brown desks. I must have been a great help to those

pupils—I taught them the rhyming scheme of the Elizabethan sonnet and how to diagram complex sentences.

The stark reality this essay conveys about the impact of the typical English language arts curriculum on students' lived experiences prompts us to ask the question, *Why do we teach what we teach?* And maybe more importantly, *How can we ensure that students get what they truly need from what we teach?* We, too, are living in unprecedented times, and with care and precision, we must consider how students' needs have shifted due to the pandemic. Although as teachers, we often do not have the power to arbitrarily change curricular topics, we *do* have the power to change the conversations in our classroom to make topics more relevant to our students' lived experiences as well as the ability to partner with them so that they have full ownership of what they are learning. Consider how conversations about respect, curiosity, compassion, forgiveness, empathy, and so on, can be woven into your curriculum and truly make an impact—the enduring ideas, knowledge, and understandings in life that are lasting and truly worth knowing.

On top of everything, we need to view our students as competent sources of knowledge and to listen attentively to what they have to say. It is our responsibility to seek out students' perspectives and develop class cultures where their viewpoints and ideas are not only valued but where their feedback informs the curriculum we teach. When students work hand in hand with teachers to shape the curriculum, they are better able to engage in more meaningful learning.

It is certain that "as public spheres, classrooms and schools are spaces in which young people construct their identities in relation to what they encounter there" (Sleeter & Carmona, 2017, p. 136). When the curriculum fosters the development of the whole child, it can support students to form positive self-images, confidence in their abilities, improved relationships with the greater world, and an overall sense of well-being. So, *talk to the kids!* Tell them *why* your teaching is important for them. Explain how it might shape their relationship with their future worlds and connect with their personal skills and unique talents. And most importantly, rethink what you are teaching if you cannot share *why* what you are teaching is important to them.

EQUITY IN ACTION

Evelyn Daza, coordinator of ENL Services, Long Beach Public Schools, New York, shared her school's work to create equitable opportunities for student learning.

Once a month at 4:00 p.m., over 40 teachers, students, administrators, board members, and community partners from the Long Beach School District attend the monthly equity committee meeting. We come together with one goal in mind—to eliminate gaps in opportunity, access, and outcomes that are predictable by a students' race, ethnicity, socioeconomic status, or any other demographic factor by examining and changing current practices, systems, and subsequent outcomes. Before the COVID pandemic, we used to meet in a large conference room; however, since the pandemic, our meetings are conducted through Zoom. Our equity committee is composed of three subcommittees: Ensuring a Culturally Responsive Curriculum, Programs that Promote Equity, and Building Community Partnerships to Ensure All Voices Are Heard.

At one recent meeting, we listened attentively to Dr. Paul Romanelli, our assistant superintendent, while he summarized the work done by the Ensuring a Culturally Responsive Curriculum subcommittee. He started by announcing the extensive purchase of literature with diverse main characters, authors, and plots for every K–12 classroom and school library to ensure our texts are representative of our student population. The room is filled with excitement as images of book covers such as The Proudest Blue, Dear Martin, and Clap When You Land embellished the slide. He also discussed shifts made to ensure that students with disabilities have access to more curricular offerings. Curriculum changes made to the algebra and living environment courses were specifically designed for English learners, and they give promise to higher New York State Regents passing rates in math and science for this subgroup. Lastly, Holocaust remembrance programs, as well as anti-bias education programs through the Anti-Defamation League, have also been implemented.

Our next step will be to survey the teaching staff using the Culturally Responsive Curriculum Scorecard designed by The Education and Justice Research and Organizing Collaborative (EJ-ROC, 2021) at New York University, Steinhardt School of Education; this tool examines the extent to which a curriculum is culturally responsive or not. The findings will lead our work in the near future. Before joining our subcommittees in the breakout rooms, our assistant superintendent reminded us that our book club starts next week, and that we will be reading, So You Want to Talk About Race (Oluo, 2019). He has set up an online platform for us to reflect on our reading and comment on after every couple of chapters. I look forward to the conversations on race and racial oppression that will ensue.

We joined our subcommittee breakout rooms for the rest of the hour. My subcommittee continued the conversation on Programs that Promote Equity. We discussed the AVID (Advancement Via Individual Determination) (www.avid.org) program implemented at the high school, which was designed to close the opportunity gap among diverse and underrepresented demographic groups. We were delighted to find that ENL students have applied since language is not a barrier to entering the program. We discussed the opening of a clothing closet and food pantry at the high school; due to the pandemic, many families have lost work and are now facing food insecurities. During the upcoming academic year, we will explore how we will bring this initiative to others in the district.

PARTING THOUGHTS

As educators, we frequently focus on what happens in the classroom—the place where we tend to have the most control. In this chapter, we have attempted to shift attention to the foundations on which classroom practices are built and address issues of equity in the curriculum through the lens of working with MLs. The pandemic undoubtedly has served as a catalyst for questioning what we teach as well as how we teach. As we move forward, let's be forever circumspect about including the voices of the marginalized and minoritized and navigating how to best integrate language and content learning for our MLs. Let's continue to raise our voices to this cause so that all MLs will be recognized for their full potential, given the necessary framework to succeed, and ultimately thrive in the classroom and beyond.

Reflections and Actions

1. In this chapter, we advocate for a critical call to action to recalibrate the curriculum to best meet the learning needs of multilingual students. How might you begin such a task? Which data might inform your decisions?

2. We have advocated for culturally responsive and sustaining teaching to be woven into all content areas as a benefit to all students, not just MLs. Where would you begin to make changes to incorporate the culture and perspectives of people whose voices have traditionally been neglected?

3. How can you design units and lessons so that students have opportunities to partner in the creation of curriculum, materials, and assignments that are relevant to them?

4. We discussed the notion of teacher clarity, activating prior knowledge and building background, academic language and literacy integration, critical thinking, and student collaboration as practices that all educators can incorporate into their teaching. In what ways might you enhance instruction by incorporating these practices?

Key Resources

Culturally Responsive Teaching and Math

Twelve Ways to Make Math More Culturally Responsive by Larry Ferlazzo (2020).

https://www.edweek.org/teaching-learning/opinion-twelve-ways-to-make-math-more-culturally-responsive/2020/12

Critical Thinking

10 Tips for Teaching Kids to Be Awesome Critical Thinkers by Mariana Martinelli (2018).

https://www.weareteachers.com/10-tips-for-teaching-kids-to-be-awesome-critical-thinkers/

75+ Critical Thinking Questions by Karen Nelson (2021).

https://www.weareteachers.com/critical-thinking-questions/

Curriculum Scorecard

The Culturally Responsive-Sustaining Scorecard by NYU Steinhardt (2019).

https://steinhardt.nyu.edu/sites/default/files/2020-12/CRE%20Scorecard%20Revised%20Aug%202020.pdf

CHAPTER 4

Teach and Assess to Build Student Autonomy, Agency, and Resilience

Have you ever seen how artists prepare their palettes: how they intentionally choose 10 or more base colors, arranging them in a particular order, readying them for mixing? Have you ever witnessed the process of how just about any hue emerges from those few basic paint dabs? If you looked closely, you would notice that the palette itself is made of some sort of thin hard material, wood most traditionally, with its smooth flat surface inviting the artist to combine the colors in near-infinite ways. There are some additional tools that are also needed, such as brushes and palette knives, aiding in blending the colors in just the right ratio. Once the careful preparation is complete, the artist lifts the palette in one hand, balancing it on their arm for easier access, and the creativity takes over.

Like painting, teaching is a form of art, so intricate, so complex, so powerful we chose the paint palette as a metaphor for the multifarious experiences teachers have daily when they prepare for instruction; design their units and lessons; make weekly, daily, and in-the-moment decisions; and most important, when they create magic.

Most educators hold bachelor or master of science degrees in education, and many of us have taken extensive course work in pedagogy, child or adolescent psychology, methods of teaching and assessment, and so forth. Yet here we liken the practice of teaching to artistry. Stay with us a little longer as we explore this metaphor: *Have you ever thought back to what happened after you joined the teaching profession and entered your first classroom? Have you perhaps observed how your pedagogy, content knowledge, and skills had gone through a creative transformation into a type of artistic expression?* We have! Let the paint palette itself stand for the solid, scientific foundation necessary for teaching to be research informed and evidence based. The palette, the brushes, and knives with all the paints are tools of the trade for the artist, just as curriculum maps, lesson plans, routines, strategies, and techniques are tools for educators. Using a paint palette, the artist approaches their task with intention and intuition, their moves carefully planned yet adjusted as needed. The genius of the artist guides the mixing of the colors, the application of the paint to the canvas, the continued movement of the paintbrush until the piece is finished; similarly, the genius of the teacher drives the choices to be made before and during the lesson, the adjustments made in the classroom, and the vision for the final project.

For so many educators, the brutal reality of the pandemic did nothing short of bringing that genius out more than ever before: creativity, resilience, and problem-solving required us to adapt to the dramatic changes as instruction shifted between and among remote, hybrid, synchronous, asynchronous, simultaneous, and face-to-face modalities for over a year. There was a marked shift to embracing the collaborative genius as well (also referred to as collective teacher efficacy, Donohoo, 2017), teachers working together remotely, combining experiences, connecting with each other locally and globally through social media, readily sharing what works and what does not, embracing a collective responsibility for all students to get through the worst of times. This chapter looks at how on the other side of the pandemic the creativity, readiness to adapt to new challenges, and willingness to redefine equitable education must continue, so we can teach multilingual learners and assess their progress while also building student autonomy, agency, and academic resilience. The work has just begun!

THE URGENCY

"Highly engaging learning opportunities such as project-based learning are critical: they even the playing field and bring in all of those talents, those skills, those desires our students have. They are learning new skills along the way, but it really is a beautiful way of tapping into their interests and abilities."

—Beth Skelton

The pandemic has challenged our students and educators in previously unfathomable ways! It disrupted our set ways, urged us to question everything we know and do, and forced us to rethink, reimagine, and retool our daily instructional and assessment practices. Before we could even consider teaching, at the beginning of the pandemic, we had to attend to children's basic survival needs: health and nutrition, safety, and well-being. When it came to planning our first lessons, we had to go way beyond simple revisions! Old lesson plans were tossed, adapted, or completely rewritten. Scope and sequence charts and pacing guides were adjusted for independent student work; unit plans were scratched to create space for social-emotional support and one-on-one guidance for students. New apps and programs filled our computer screens, and learning about technology integration flooded our foggy brains.

We were all first-year teachers during the pandemic, surviving personally and professionally but also transforming our daily work and ensuring that our students not just survived but thrived. But what have we truly learned? More specifically, what have we learned about teaching and assessing multilingual learners (MLs) amid the changes? We have spoken with, coached, and supported numerous teachers in the past year who overwhelmingly agree with us—multilinguals are brave, resilient, hard-working, and curious children and youths, most of whom have found their own ways or were lovingly supported by their teachers, families, and communities to develop and enact their agency, autonomy, and resilience and are coming out stronger on the other side of the pandemic. Others needed and will continue to need our heightened awareness of their complex realities, tragedies and losses, patience, and multifaceted support system (see Chapter 5 for more). We must intentionally work together to welcome students back where they are, not where they could, should, or would have been. Let's not waste our time pathologizing or trying to fix the students as if they had been broken or shattered; instead, let's pause to ensure they feel fully supported as they adjust to a changing, evolving, still very volatile life filled with uncertainties. Before we make a stronger case as to why agency, autonomy, and resilience are essential dimensions of equitable instruction and assessment, let's define what these terms mean for MLs in the context of teaching, learning, and assessment.

- **Agency** is a multilingual learner's ability to take an active role in defining their own short-term and long-term academic, linguistic, and personal goals and to pursue those goals purposefully and successfully.
  - Agency does not mean leaving students to their own devices in the midst of a crisis or allowing them to sink or swim without guidance or to feel overwhelmed by choices.

- **Autonomy** is a multilingual learner's ability to develop independence and respond to academic, linguistic, and personal challenges by applying their spirit, talent, knowledge, and skills to new situations.
  - Autonomy is not achieved by requiring independence and self-reliance by simply assigning difficult work to students and then leaving them to figure it out on their own.

- **Resilience** is a multilingual learner's ability to learn to manage adverse academic, social, linguistic, and personal experiences and to develop coping strategies regarding whatever challenges or obstacles they must face in and outside the classroom.
  - Resilience does not mean ignoring the suffering, pain, loss, or stress the pandemic caused to our students or families directly or indirectly, nor is it to expect any student to just toughen up, pull themselves up by their bootstraps, or cope without support.

Now, more than ever, we share an urgent need to reconfigure our beliefs about educating MLs. Equitable and effective teaching is much more than covering the curriculum, delivering instruction, and assigning and grading tasks. In Bettina Love's (2020) words, "We must radically dream because before COVID-19 closed our schools and dismantled our way of life, schools were failing not only children of color but all children" (para. 2). Multilingual learners have been impacted by inequitable access to resources and learning opportunities, low expectations, discriminatory assessment practices, and few role models that reflect their personal images and backgrounds for too long. The time has come to *radically dream* and create equity in our classrooms for MLs and for ALLs (academic language learners) (Ottow, 2019; Soto-Hinman & Hetzel, 2009). This chapter will reveal how to build student autonomy, agency, and resilience to do just that.

STUDENT PORTRAITS

At the onset of the pandemic, Johanna's father worked in a neighboring state, and her mother fell ill with the coronavirus within weeks. Her hospitalization brought aunts, neighbors, and others together to figure out a rotation to help care for the children. Johanna, a third grader, found herself at home alone a lot with her older sister, Angélica, in fifth grade, and younger brother, Romero, still in kindergarten, all sitting around the kitchen table trying to keep up with the packets sent home, figuring out the Chromebooks dropped off by the bus driver one day, keeping busy and fighting fear, fatigue, and boredom all at the same time.

Johanna discovered a special way to keep herself busy. She started doodling, drawing pictures, and writing about her days, her wishes, her fears, her mom and dad. She mainly wrote in English since she never went to a bilingual class or learned to read and write in Spanish, even though the house was filled with conversations in Spanish—the sound of Spanish from the television, as well as neighbors and relatives, visiting. Johanna kept interrupting her sister, begging her to teach her how to write in Spanish, too. Angélica did not want to be bothered at first; she felt overwhelmed trying to look after her younger brother, too, but the nagging of her sister was too much, so she finally gave in. After about two weeks, the two girls were often found huddling over the notebook designated to capture sketches of their daily realities, their thoughts in Spanish and English, and some random drawings, including geometric patterns and other dazzling images that calmed the mind. They called it *El Libro, The Book*.

Markers, crayons, glitter glue, stickers, and paint with brushes of a few sizes all came out one at a time. The daily entries into *The Book* included notes about their mom getting better, their father hoping to come to see them as soon as possible, reminders of what to add to the next shopping list, and wish lists about what life after the pandemic may look like. Some days, the book was left untouched; on others, it consumed an hour of their time to write and draw in it. They took pictures from the pages of *The Book* and texted them to their mother—who was enduring an excruciatingly long and uncertain hospital stay without seeing any family members—adding voice messages and made-up songs and chants in Spanish and English as well. Occasionally, they included their little brother by reading a page or two to him, but they preferred to keep *El Libro* their secret.

Johanna and Angélica did not know the technical term for it, but they discovered a way not only to survive but thrive. They used their tools of creativity, autonomy, and agency to get through the toughest times of their lives. How did *El Libro* make a difference? It was their personal experiences and their desire to express themselves in multiple ways, multiple languages, and multiple modalities that kept the girls meaningfully engaged. They connected with each other through shared language and literacy practices; connected artistic and linguistic representations of their thoughts and feelings; and found joy, comfort, and reassurance in learning together and sharing that experience with their family members.

Let's stop and critically reflect on Johanna and her siblings' experiences in light of the concepts of autonomy, agency, and resilience we introduced prior to this vignette.

Let's look back through the student portrait and find evidence of each by pondering these questions:

- How have Johanna and her sister Angélica developed autonomy?

- How has *EL Libro* contributed to their agency as readers and writers?

- In what ways do Johanna's family embody resilience?

- Do you see these same characteristics in MLs in your classrooms? If so, what might have supported their development? If not, how can you try to nurture these qualities?

- What was happening with the little brother? He is largely absent from the story, so what could be or should be done to support his autonomy, agency, and resilience at such a young age?

LOOKING BACK, LOOKING AHEAD

Focusing on student agency, autonomy, and resilience in the academic context is not new. Advocates for educating the whole child (ASCD, 2021) and infusing social-emotional learning into daily instructional practices have promoted research, theory, and practice in support of helping students "develop healthy identities, manage emotions and achieve personal and collective goals, feel and show empathy for others, establish and maintain supportive relationships, and make responsible and caring decisions" (CASEL, 2021, para. 2). On the other hand, multilingual learners and their families have relied on their personal and collective strengths as well as creative problem-solving to survive against all odds, in the face of severe adversity, long before the pandemic. Many MLs' immediate or extended families who are new to this country have encountered multiple stressors of the immigrant experience, some of which include (a) the trauma of leaving their homeland and resettling somewhere new; (b) the prolonged time it often takes to secure jobs, to establish new routines, and to stabilize family life; (c) the process of acculturation; (d) the rejections that come from racial, linguistic, or faith-based discrimination; and (e) the anti-immigrant sentiments, biases, and occasionally the violence.

Let's pause before we return to the new school year and make a commitment to fully dismantle and disrupt the type of teaching and assessment practices that hurt MLs, render them second-class citizens, and even with the best of intention, contribute to not just achievement disparities but daily opportunity gaps. Let's emerge from the pandemic with unapologetic advocacy for equity for MLs and offer counternarratives that reveal how these students lived through history and what they *can do.* Let's create compassionate, engaging, learning spaces where collective healing and perseverance shape our pedagogy while we pursue academic excellence and equity for all students. The lessons learned in the past year cannot go to waste; we are at a historic moment to reevaluate and reimagine our instructional and assessment practices for equity for MLs. Looking forward, let's begin or (for those who have already begun this work) continue to:

- Remind MLs daily that we genuinely care for them and support their holistic development, including their academic, linguistic, and social-emotional growth. At the same time, remind *yourself* that no score, label, or single grade should or could ever define a child.

- Value our students' personal and shared stories and experiences.

- Create and sustain (in-class or virtual) spaces for learning driven by student curiosity, passion, and interest.

- Offer choices of pathways to learning, resources, and materials that are equally rigorous, tap into student interests, and immerse students in authentic, real-world tasks.

- Honor and uplift all voices and forms of self-expression.

- Celebrate the independence and autonomy MLs gained through countless remote and asynchronous hours of learning and further hone traditional as well as new modes of communication that keep them front and center in the learning process.

- Ensure all forms of learning and language development are joyful and affirming.

- Learn *from, about,* and *with* our students by redefining and celebrating teaching and learning as a joint, collaborative process in which *students are teachers and teachers are learners.*

When we consistently apply these actions, we create the conditions for MLs to become self-directed, independent learners who embrace their agency and autonomy and strengthen their resilience toward adverse experiences. Let's agree to teach and assess in ways that amplify MLs' talents, enable them to fulfill their potential, enhance their academic and linguistic progress, and inspire them to be leaders of their own learning. How do we translate these understandings and commitments into daily practices? How do we plan for equity in teaching and assessment? Try the following self-reflection and goal-setting tool to get started.

> *Use this self-reflection and goal-setting tool to assess what is part of your practice already and how you can commit to take action:*

- ☐ Take time to learn about and incorporate students' lived experiences from the perspectives of the pandemic.

- ☐ Invite students to tell their story and offer a new narrative of their experiences, their cultures, and histories.

- ☐ Ask students about their takeaways from the past year.

- ☐ Survey students to learn about their learning strengths and preferences.

- ☐ Have students set their own learning goals.

- ☐ Encourage and validate in- and out-of-class experiences that foster authentic language use (any language) in oral and written communication.

- ☐ Establish routines that continue to include technology, even when students are back in school (teacher- and student-created, recorded, multimedia materials; multimodal response system that includes students recording themselves; and virtual synchronous and asynchronous interactions, such as discussion boards or breakout rooms.

- ☐ Plan for breaking down and never watering down new learning for MLs.

- ☐ Schedule frequent check-ins with students and their families (see Chapter 5 for more).

- ☐ Coach your MLs for student-led conferences to monitor their own progress and set goals.

- ☐ Make project-based, problem-based, and performance-based assessments your go-to approaches for gauging mastery of content learning, as well as language and literacy development.

LET'S TEACH THE WAY STUDENTS LEARN

How multilingual learners experience the world and develop conceptual understanding, as well as their multiple language and literacy practices are both similar and distinct in many ways when compared to their monolingual peers. As their educators, our first responsibility is to recognize and advocate for multilingualism: Being bilingual or multilingual is an asset and has no detriment to students' content and English language development. Just the opposite! Numerous studies discuss the *bilingual advantage*, and ample anecdotal evidence exists to support what a gift it is to communicate in more than one language. Multilingual students learn and process information in multiple languages and multiple modalities and through personal, familial, community-based experiences as well as through powerful teaching that scaffolds up rather than oversimplifies new learning (Nordmeyer et al., 2021).

From experience and research, we also know that MLs need to and can develop academic language through active participation in multidimensional learning opportunities (MacDonald et al., 2020). Language and literacy should never be considered a prerequisite to participating in any grade-level instruction; instead, language and literacy develop when they are authentically embedded in engaging classroom activities that have the following characteristics:

- Ample experiential, hands-on learning opportunities
  - Learning by doing
  - Showing not just telling students
  - Providing hands-on and digital-based activities
  - Connect with and showcase guest speakers and experts that are culturally and linguistically diverse and will allow students to see themselves and their community represented
- A culture of inquiry based on students' natural curiosity
  - Students asking authentic questions
  - Students sharing their noticings and wonderings
  - Lessons built on student interest and intrinsic motivation
- Ensuring students personally connect with lessons
  - Challenging, thought-provoking prompts, scenarios, and so forth
  - Using elements of surprise, humor, stories, art, music, and movement
  - Surprising students with learning moments that make learning memorable
- Learning options
  - Allowing for choices in how students tackle problems
  - Encouraging students to use multiple languages and resources
  - Varying grouping configurations
- Amplifying student voice through discussions
  - Dynamic, varied student interactions
  - Opportunities for collaborative exploration

We must also recognize that "multilingual learners draw on their metacognitive, metalinguistic, and metacultural awareness to develop effectiveness in language use" (WIDA, 2020, p. 12). We can't take this for granted or make any assumptions. Many bilingual and multilingual people of all ages intuitively compare, evaluate, and reflect on cultural, linguistic, and cognitive experiences as they negotiate meaning-making across academic and non-academic situations. For example, consider a student—who recently arrived from another country and another educational system—who witnesses someone in class interrupting the teacher to ask a question or contradicting the teacher by sharing a different point of view. Reflecting on such discourse, the student might at first be confused or even appalled by such behavior, considering such actions to be disrespectful, argumentative, and rude. From this encounter, the student may make assumptions about how teachers can be spoken to and actually use language that is too familiar or impolite. It is vitally important to understand why students speak and act the way they do before making any judgments.

When we recognize these dimensions of our own teaching and when we explicitly model our own metacognitive, metalinguistic, and metacultural processes for students, they benefit in multiple ways: Students get to see and hear examples of thinking *about thinking*, thinking *about language*, and thinking about *one's cultural identity*.

TAKING INSPIRATION FROM THE STUDENTS

To build student autonomy, agency, and resilience, let's make sure we are not just teaching our multilingual students, but we also take every opportunity to learn *from* and *with* them. When we define our roles as guides and facilitators and when we are intentional about the instructional choices we make based on student input, student feedback, and student interest, the teaching-learning process goes through a transformation.

- **Find out and build on** what the students can already do and what knowledge and skills they already have, both related and unrelated to the content you are teaching.
  - For example, find out what your students are passionate about and what they do outside of school. For immigrant youth, learn about the school system and the curriculum and pedagogy the students and their families come from.

- **Embrace learning** as your primary role—teach to learn and learn to teach honoring multiple points of view.
  - For example, frequently invite your students to co-construct lessons with you by centering lessons on their questions and goals and by co-creating assessment measures and tools (such as rubrics).

- **Affirm** the multiple realities and experiences multilingual students have with cognition, learning processes, linguistic repertoires, and ways of expression.
  - For example, be specific and supportive of students without becoming too generic or patronizing. Offer actionable feedback and concrete praise, "You're doing such a good job on that project," is not as meaningful as, "I observed you working with your group and you collaborate really well. How did you learn that?"

- **Make MLs feel comfortable** asking challenging questions, critically examining ideas presented in class, and sharing new perspectives.

- For example, model high expectations for critical thinking, appropriate ways to challenge authority, engage in dialogue around key controversial issues, and nurture criticality in the learning process (Muhammad, 2020).

LET'S TEACH THE WAY STUDENTS CAN SUCCEED

MLs are frequently placed in programs that provide either discontinuous access to general education content or their instruction is completely unconnected to grade-level subjects. *What if we had no more disjointed, fragmented teaching? What if, instead, we integrated content, language, literacy, and social-emotional learning (SEL)?* As things go, the ultimate goal for students is to give up dependency and become independent learners (Hammond, 2015), so we must simultaneously support and challenge MLs (Snyder & Staehr Fenner, 2021) to meet the grade-level benchmarks that are set in all subject areas.

Let's make a commitment to:

1. Offer multimodal, multisensory, and multilingual access to the core content so MLs would be able to not just have a basic understanding but mastery of the grade-appropriate content, even if they do not yet have full command of the subject matter in English.

2. Systematically examine the core content curriculum for language features that are critical to understanding, developing, and ultimately mastering, so *all* students may be able to actively engage in the lessons.

3. Honor multiliteracies and multiple representations.

4. Assess what the students can do and meet them where they are.

5. Design lessons that acknowledge students' backgrounds and identities.

6. Ensure that all visitors to the classroom—either in-person or online— understand the inclusive philosophy of your students, including co-teachers, parents, principals, school counselors, guests.

EQUITY-INFORMED, INTEGRATED APPROACHES TO PLANNING INSTRUCTION FOR MLS

In this book, we center instructional practices on the needs of multilingual learners. We recognize that many additional factors must be addressed in order to create a fully equitable learning experience for MLs (such as human and material resources, access to new academic materials rather than discarded leftovers). Here we remain focused on the instructional and assessment choices teachers make and how they can teach and assess for equity by applying multiple lenses (that is, cognitive, linguistic, and social-emotional) to their lessons:

1. The **cognitive lens** ensures that academic rigor and core content expectations are at the forefront of what we teach. Students' language proficiency levels must not be used as a predictor of whether or not they are capable of cognitively engaging with academic content and skills: Let's commit to providing equitable, engaging, challenging, culturally, historically, and linguistically responsive and sustaining content instruction across all grade level and all curricular areas to our MLs. Among others, Aida Walqui (2020) has been advocating for an approach to teaching MLs built on the *high rigor, high support* principle, according to which instruction is amplified and not simplified.

2. The **linguistic lens** allows for an explicit examination of the academic language and literacy opportunities and expectations embedded in all classes. The linguistic lens requires us to not only consider academic language and literacy demands and expectations that are hidden in plain sight in every lesson but turn them into complex yet authentic opportunities for engaging in language and literacy practices.

3. The **social-emotional lens** urges us not to overlook how our MLs (a) navigate their own emotions and aspirations; (b) build relationships with others, including learning about perspective-taking and collaborating; and (c) defining their place in the world. Daniel Goleman and Peter Senge (2014) call this the triple focus on three skill sets representing the *inner,* the *other,* and the *outer* spheres of our existence. The pandemic intensified the need to never ignore this dimension of our students' learning and well-being in the future!

Figure 4.1 offers ample examples of how to plan instruction through the three lenses to help magnify equity goals for MLs so they, too, can fully participate in learning within the classroom and engage in academic tasks to their full potential, be it with their peers or on their own. If our agreed-upon commitment is to increase MLs' autonomy, agency, and resilience and our ultimate goal is to create equity for MLs, then plan instructions that build independence with processes of content, language, literacy, and social-emotional learning.

Are you wondering why this would all be necessary or how this approach to teaching contributes to MLs' development of agency, autonomy, and resilience? Let's put the idea to the test. Revisit Figure 4.1 and analyze each point made with these three guiding questions:

1. *Are students going to develop more ownership of their learning and agency?*

2. *Are MLs going to increase their independence and autonomy as capable learners?*

3. *Are MLs going to persevere, take risks, and seek resources, such as ask their peers before asking for help from a teacher or simply giving up?*

You might also be wondering how this will all fit into any one lesson or even unit. Our strongest argument is that by virtue of focusing on equity and using multiple lenses for lesson planning, we become more reflective about our students' needs, engage in deeper professional dialogue with

FIGURE 4.1 ● Summary of Three Lenses for Lesson Integration

LENS	HOW EDUCATORS PLAN FOR EQUITY FOR MLS
Cognitive (Based on Krathwol, 2002; Yilmaz, 2011)	Rather than focusing on what facts MLs need to understand and remember, consider how they can apply, analyze, and evaluate information.
	Consider what the big ideas are in a unit of study: What is the essential learning to be transferred to the next unit *and* to future learning, including real-life problems?
	Consider how MLs may participate in learning activities and interactions to have access to and develop mastery of the procedures by offering the right amount of support and nurturing independence.
	Connect new learning to MLs' metacognitive, metalinguistic, and metacultural awareness by encouraging deep reflection about their own learning.
	Guide students in identifying their own learning goals, establishing learning strategies, and engaging in self-assessment.
Linguistic (Nordmeyer et al., 2021; WIDA, 2020)	Address all three dimensions of how language is used at the word, sentence, and discourse levels for academic purposes and highlight what is unique about academic language use within each core discipline.
	Offer verbal and written scaffolds when needed. Allow for multilingual responses. Invite multiple modes of expression (verbal and nonverbal, visual representations).
	Guide students through structured mini-lessons that explicitly teach literacy skills while also engaging students in authentic, joyful opportunities to use their multiple literacies for self-expression.
	Capitalize on MLs' ability to access their full linguistic repertoires and activate awareness of how they use their languages across different contexts.
Social-Emotional (Based on CASEL, 2019)	Nurture growth mindset. Celebrate MLs and ensure they fully believe in themselves. Help MLs develop self-confidence in a new learning environment and in a new language. Recognize MLs for their competence.
	Encourage self-advocacy. Teach stress-management techniques. Help develop skills to overcome adverse circumstances.
	Develop empathy and respect for others. Assist students' understanding of others who come from a range of racial, cultural, and linguistic backgrounds.
	Advance students' understanding of verbal and nonverbal social cues. Develop conflict resolution and problem-solving skills. Develop trust in others. Experience a school and classroom climate where risk-taking is the norm without fear of ridicule or embarrassment.
	Encourage cognitive and social-emotional flexibility and tolerance for ambiguity. Practice creative problem-solving.

each other, and show that we are committed to our students' growth and equitable development in all these dimensions. Content and language integration is a fairly well-established practice. Adding a social-emotional focus to planning takes us beyond the dichotomy of content and language goals or objectives and ensures students' affective connections to learning. At the core of all this are student voice, active participation, and critical engagement—engagement with the content, with academic language and literacy practices, and with students' and their peers' authentic selves. As suggested by Kibler and her colleagues (2021), "critical and dialogic educational practices provide a space for students to learn through multiple voices and perspectives" (p. xiii). Students need to talk in any language of their choice: talk to other children and youth, talk to English-speaking peers and same-language partners, and talk to their teachers and other adults in the classroom and school environment. They cannot be silent or silenced. Within the content classes, they also need to actively participate in academic conversations with peer and teacher guidance and support. Here are some examples of how to do that across the four core content areas and beyond (please note that these tips can be transferred to other contexts and content areas):

- In math, engage students in math talk and draw special attention to (a) the way students explain their thinking and (b) the precision of language needed to fully engage in disciplinary practices.

- In social studies, have students pose their own questions, establish their own line of inquiry, and participate in respectful debates and critical conversations around issues students sincerely care about.

- In science, engage students in task-based discussions that build on hands-on explorations and multiple representations, such as diagrams, outlines, sketches, and video-recorded responses as well as in inquiry that provides additional opportunities for oracy.

- In language arts, select nonfiction and fiction pieces to discuss that are relevant to students' lives and invite students to share their own examples; use "pairing" strategies that simultaneously introduce the informational/nonfiction and fiction versions of a topic; and embrace multiliteracies as you explore multimedia resources, video clips, and films in addition to print-based materials.

- In music, invite students to share personal and cultural experiences with music and songs related to the lesson.

- In visual arts, have students describe both their plans for their work, the processes they engaged in, and share their final products.

Why is this so important? "By providing multiple opportunities for students to negotiate meaning in disciplinary conversation together, we can engage multilingual learners in the interactions that, over time and with appropriate modeling, enable them to become increasingly effective in expressing and exploring ideas" (Nordmeyer et al., 2021, p. 65). Sustained, authentic, and well-supported academic conversations coupled with similarly sustained, authentic, and well-supported writing, reading, and listening opportunities pave the way to equitable classroom experiences for MLs. See the checklist below to guide your reflection and self-assessment of your planning and instruction:

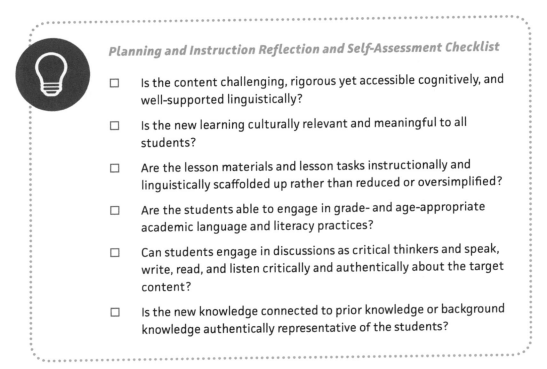

Planning and Instruction Reflection and Self-Assessment Checklist

☐ Is the content challenging, rigorous yet accessible cognitively, and well-supported linguistically?

☐ Is the new learning culturally relevant and meaningful to all students?

☐ Are the lesson materials and lesson tasks instructionally and linguistically scaffolded up rather than reduced or oversimplified?

☐ Are the students able to engage in grade- and age-appropriate academic language and literacy practices?

☐ Can students engage in discussions as critical thinkers and speak, write, read, and listen critically and authentically about the target content?

☐ Is the new knowledge connected to prior knowledge or background knowledge authentically representative of the students?

TALK WITH AND LISTEN TO YOUR STUDENTS

Hugs, handshakes, or high-fives might not be coming back soon, but building relational trust and authentic connections with our students will be more important than ever. Let's talk to our multilingual learners and hear them share about where they have been and where they are going with their learning. Let's pause for it to sink in what former superintendent, Theresa Thayer Snyder (2020) cautions us about:

> When the children return to school, they will have returned with a new history that we will need to help them identify and make sense of. When the children return to school, we will need to listen to them. Let their stories be told. They have endured a year that has no parallel in modern times. There is no assessment that applies to who they are or what they have learned. (para. 2)

We, too, suggest that we listen to our students, let them share their experiences, and recognize the historic times we have lived through. Ample one-on-one conversations and small-group conferencing time will allow our students to tell their stories and engage in continued dialogue about their progress. Whatever platform you choose, face-to-face discussions or dialogue journaling, these informal ways of uncovering what the students are thinking about, what they are grappling with, and what they are truly curious to learn about will be more beneficial than any quiz or test score. Ask them questions and invite them to ask you! Find out what they missed, what they gained, and what they need moving forward in the new academic year, in a new course, or in a new unit. To support their agency, talk to your students about how they can personally relate to the learning across content areas and invite them to determine why they are learning what they are learning and why it matters. To support their autonomy, encourage your students to take pride in their content, language, and literacy development and ask them to share ways they have persevered and worked through problems while also seeking help when needed. To support their resilience, encourage positive self-talk and discuss questions, such as what they are saying to themselves and what they are thinking to themselves when they face a new challenge.

EQUITABLE ASSESSMENT PRACTICES

We share a core belief that everything we do in the classroom is driven by relationships and interactions that take place in the classroom and school community. Assessment practices are no different. As suggested by Margo Gottlieb and Andrea Honigsfeld, "approaches to assessment are relationship driven, primarily among students (in assessment *as* learning), teachers (in assessment *for* learning), and school leaders (in assessment *of* learning)" (Calderón et al., 2020, p. 143). Since in this book we primarily focus on classroom-based teaching and assessment practices, these three approaches to assessments are summarized in Figure 4.2, with examples of what equity-focused approaches, teacher and student actions, and appropriate tools are for day-to-day instructional choices. Our overarching goal is to clear some pathways with the following in mind:

- To overcome the tension between some pre-existing beliefs about what MLs can or cannot do or should or should not do

- To allow the students' work to speak for them by examining student work samples without bias or preconceived notions

- To explore evidence of student learning collaboratively (with colleagues and students) by inviting students to show not just tell us (via formal or traditional assessments) what they know or can do within the context of content, language, literacy, and social-emotional learning

Addressing inequities and possible solutions related to large-scale standardized assessments and reforming grading policies and practices are

FIGURE 4.2 ● Summary of Approaches to Assessment With Associated Equity-Focused Teacher and Learner Actions and Examples of Tools

APPROACHES TO ASSESSMENT	EQUITY-FOCUSED COLLABORATIVE TEACHERS ACTIONS	MULTILINGUAL LEARNER ACTIONS	EXAMPLES OF TOOLS FOR ASSESSMENT EQUITY
Assessment as Learning	Create opportunities for self- and peer-assessment and peer-feedback Guide students to self-monitor their own learning Encourage students to take responsibility for their work and develop independence Help students document their growth and show evidence of their learning	Engage in self- and peer-assessment Set short-term and long-term goals Advocate for themselves by explaining their own learning processes, strengths, and needs Reflect on own learning progress	Utilized by students • Self- and peer-assessment rubrics and rating scales • Peer-editing checklists • Learning logs • Interactive/dialogue journals • Reflection tools
Assessment for Learning	Co-construct success criteria carefully aligned to learning intentions Co-create a menu of formative assessment tasks to encourage student choice Determine the most culturally and linguistically appropriate formative assessment data collection methods Use data from previous formative assessment measures to plan instruction	Contribute to constructing success criteria Understand and articulate own learning goals and intentions Contribute to assessment choice menus and rubrics Purposefully choose assessment tasks to demonstrate learning progress Advocate for next steps in instruction	Utilized by teachers and students • Graphic organizers • Checklists • Rubrics or project descriptors • Templates of criteria for success • Action research, along with reflection tools
Assessment of Learning	Review and update student portraits with summative data Review unit goals and desired outcomes and create multidimensional assessment tasks that are multimodal, multilingual, and allow for multiple ways of demonstrating (progress toward) mastery Consider how standards and assessments are aligned to students' short-term and long-term needs	Contribute to student portrait Contribute to end-of-unit performance or project rubrics Choose end-of-unit assessment tasks (performance- or project-based assessments) Create, analyze, and reflect on student-created portfolios Use standards to monitor progress and set short-term and long-term learning goals	Utilized by administrators and school leaders, often with teachers Communicated to students, parents, and caregivers • Data from student portraits • End-of-unit rubrics and narratives • School or district portfolios

beyond the scope of this book (see the resources section at the end of this chapter).

When assessment as, for, and of learning is collaborative in nature, it ensures a multidimensional approach not only to assessment practices embraced by educators but by their multilingual students as well. When we use an equity lens and systematically examine how we assess and how we determine what students can do, our MLs further practice their agency, autonomy, and plan accordingly; you create a more equitable learning environment for all.

Stop and reflect on how assessment practices may be connected to student agency, autonomy, and resilience in your classroom by finishing these reflection starters:

My multilingual students practice their agency when they _____

_____.

My multilingual students practice their autonomy when they _____

_____.

My multilingual students' academic, linguistic, and social-emotional resilience is nurtured when they _____.

EQUITY IN ACTION

Elizabeth Choi, ELL teacher at Farragut Middle School in Knoxville, Tennessee, expressed to us her and her students' experiences of sharing new learning during the pandemic and looking forward to moving as follows:

It is as if a veil has been lifted from the school walls and hallways. We have always focused on the needs of students at school, but now we seek to include the needs at home. Meeting those foundational needs (access to food, health care, Internet, technology, belonging, and a quiet place to study) is key to educating our English learners. With COVID, we had to give up so much: I gave up proximity to my students, both online and in the classroom. I also had to sacrifice my favorite grouping techniques. But we gained creative and persevering spirits, and we found a common ground as both teachers and students became learners (and often the roles were reversed!) The greatest lessons I have learned in this pandemic school year have come from my students. They are my best teachers and my strongest resource. I am in awe of their relentless initiative to troubleshoot finicky technology. Early in the semester, one of my virtual students had trouble submitting her math assignments through the online learning platform. This student was an English learner with a learning disability, so our initial assumptions were that he faced a challenge following the teacher's carefully crafted tutorial. However, when we arranged for the student to receive assistance at school, I discovered the problem was that her device's interface did not match the interface on the teacher's video. The directions the teacher gave were impossible to follow on her computer. We laughed as we both learned something that day! This is such a frequent disconnect that many learning platforms feature a "Student View" option so teachers can understand what our learners will see before we present a lesson. This analogy translates perfectly to the classroom. When we view our instruction through the lens of the student view, we will approach our planning with student needs and interests in mind while considering what obstacles we may inadvertently be creating. We must also pay attention to the skills our students already possess. I have one student whom we have dubbed "The King of Hacks" as he is constantly piping up in class to say, "You know, teacher, there's a better way to do that." Even though I consider myself proficient in technology, he has taught me there is always something to learn. The benefit of welcoming this exchange into the classroom is that I can respond, "You showed me how to upload that file faster; let me show you how to strengthen that introduction to your essay." I no longer have to sell a tale of how one day the student will be thankful he learned how to write an introduction. Instead, a culture exists where we embrace learning in all forms, and as a result, all who have input are valued. I do not have to elaborate on the relevance of the content because all learning is relevant. As educators approaching a post-pandemic era, we must lead by example and model the pursuit of a growth mindset by taking our own seats at the learner's table. This year my students have watched me invite and embrace struggle. Now I find that they are more willing to accept the challenges of the content and curriculum, and this sets the stage for a grand performance.

PARTING THOUGHTS

When multilingual learners grow their confidence in their academic and linguistic abilities, they work through challenging tasks, problems, and assignments with more clarity and focus and they develop a sense of agency. As thoughtful and reflective students, they learn to express their choices and preferences and are courageous and determined to advocate for themselves as learners. If they are provided ample opportunity to engage in project-based, problem-based, or inquiry-based learning, they learn to work both collaboratively and individually and learn to seek out resources (including support from peers and teachers). As they establish personal learning pathways, with the *just-in-time* and *just-right* supports, they grow in their motivation and autonomy. When MLs recognize how obstacles and challenges lead to new learning rather than giving up, giving in, or feeling all-around defeated, they strengthen their resilience. Resilience best develops within the context of trusting relationships (see Chapter 5 for more).

Reflections and Actions

1. Early in this chapter, we suggest that multilingual learners experience the world and develop conceptual understanding, as well as their multiple language and literacy practices in ways that are both similar and distinct when compared to their monolingual peers. What evidence do you have from your own teaching to support both parts of this claim?

2. Throughout the chapter, we build a case for agency, autonomy, and resilience to be recognized as essential dimensions of equitable instruction and assessment for multilingual learners. What were your beliefs about these three constructs prior to reading the chapter, and how do you plan to move forward focusing on these qualities?

3. How do integrating content, language, and social-emotional learning contribute to equitable instructional practices for MLs?

4. Some say that educators often find themselves data rich but information poor. What strategies from this chapter can you use to make sure you feel information rich about your MLs?

5. How do you create equity in assessment that supports MLs' agency, autonomy, and resilience? Use the prompts that follow to reflect on or discuss with your colleagues (a) how you engaged in fair and equitable assessment *as, for,* and *of* learning in the past, (b) in what ways your practices shifted over the pandemic, and (c) what goals and future direction you are setting for yourself.

I. *Through ongoing assessment* **as** *learning, I invite my students to look within themselves, self-assess, reflect, set their own goals, and periodically participate in this cycle.*

PAST PRACTICES	PANDEMIC PRACTICES	CURRENT PRACTICES	GOALS FOR THE FUTURE

II. *Through ongoing assessment* **for** *learning, my colleagues and I collaborate with our students to continuously search for what MLs can do, what they need in the moment to make steady progress, and how we can adjust the learning experiences to better meet their needs.*

PAST PRACTICES	PANDEMIC PRACTICES	CURRENT PRACTICES	GOALS FOR THE FUTURE

III. *Through systematic assessment* **of** *learning, my colleagues, students, and I collect, review, and reflect on information gained from multiple sources about student mastery.*

PAST PRACTICES	PANDEMIC PRACTICES	CURRENT PRACTICES	GOALS FOR THE FUTURE

Key Resources

A go-to resource on culturally responsive teaching: Snyder, S., & Staehr Fenner, D. (2021). *Culturally responsive teaching for multilingual learners: Tools for equity*. Corwin. Also see its companion website:

https://resources.corwin.com/culturallyresponsiveteaching

Colorin Colorado blogposts, interviews, articles on related topics:
https://www.colorincolorado.org/

Tan Huynh's website:
https://www.empoweringells.com/

ETS Guidelines on Assessing MLs:
https://www.ets.org/s/about/pdf/ell_guidelines.pdf

CHAPTER 5

Harness the Power of Connections and Relationships

Have you ever considered the characteristics of the complex entities and connections that make up a natural ecosystem? How do the myriads of living and nonliving components constantly interact for the benefit of all? What does the ecosystem need to not only survive but function well and thrive? In this chapter, we use the metaphor of an ecosystem to describe our schools, classrooms, and communities. Each classroom is its own dynamic and naturally multifaceted environment consisting of many multidimensional components working together. Every school, district, and community must work as a system as well. Through imbalances and change, classrooms must evolve to maintain healthy, productive, and resilient conditions.

Ecosystems are individual communities, each different in its diversity and unique in its composition. The parts of the ecosystem work interdependently to support and maintain balance and strength within the environment while evolving and adapting to ever-changing needs. Environmental scientists have demonstrated that ecosystems with more biodiversity seem to withstand disturbances with greater resistance and resilience!

The metaphor of an ecosystem and its alignment to classrooms and larger school environments portray the relationships, structures, and processes necessary for students, teachers, administrators, volunteers, and all personnel to thrive in their environment and to create a strong sense of belonging in the community. Safe and supportive classroom and school environments function through the powerful connections all members of the community build together. These connections are complex, intricate, and essential to the dynamic nature and health of all individuals in it; yet building relationships takes time! The climate of the classroom environment sets the tone for how these connections are made, how trust is established, and how relationships are built through asset-focused approaches and equitable practices that impact everyone in the larger school community as well. Although classrooms and schools are composed of multiple moving and ever-evolving parts, the parts are interconnected and interdependent. Just like an ecosystem, if one part is unhealthy or inequitable, the overall well-being of the system can be compromised.

Consider your classroom for a moment and reflect on the following:

- How do multilingual learners (MLs) navigate their surroundings?

- What can all members of the classroom and school community do to ensure they, too, have a strong sense of belonging?

- How do the workings of your classroom directly impact other classrooms within the same grade, at different grade levels, across multiple subjects, in specialty areas for enrichment and intervention services, and vice versa?

- What part do you play in your environment and the broader, more robust schoolwide system?

- Who and what influences the systems and the people within them?

THE URGENCY

"My primary goal has been relationships: maintaining relationships, maintaining connections, everyone has my home phone number, email, and WhatsApp, and I am even learning how to use social media in a safe way so that we can stay connected."

—Yuriko Gray

As previously discussed within this book, attending to students' overall academic, linguistic, and social-emotional well-being will be paramount as we welcome students into our classrooms once again and ensure they continue to learn in a physical or blended environment. Social-emotional learning (SEL) has been a hot topic in education for a number of years, but as Dena Simmons (2021) cautions, SEL without cultural competence and anti-racist education is not enough. There have been several success stories highlighting the benefits of SEL with students of all ages—however, not all schools have adopted and implemented SEL practices with multilingual students and with a unique focus on racial healing in mind. We will address strategies for culturally responsive and sustaining SEL later in this chapter. The overarching theme of the chapter is how strong connections and relationships lead to positive classroom communities and intersections of health and well-being throughout school environments to help MLs overcome adversity and trauma caused not only by COVID-19 but often by generational pain and injustices as well. This pandemic bore witness to the inequities that have existed within our communities, the long-standing disconnects that occurred, and how they have magnified the disproportionate impacts on diverse and marginalized student populations and their families, especially MLs.

Schools are supposed to be a consistent and stable environment for students and educators. Are they though, for all? When you last walked into a school building, what were some lasting impressions? Did the lights shine on the multiple bulletin board displays along the corridors displaying students' work and showcasing their talent in multiple ways celebrating diversity? Were the offices filled with people who engaged in deep conversations about the students? Did you hear chatter and sounds of joyful learning coming from classrooms? Or perhaps, the smell of food wafted through the halls from the cafeteria? Most days, we know what to expect within these walls; what makes schools special places for all members of the community are the relationships and connections we have to the people here. In the school setting, most students respond well to people who work hard and are deeply committed to building rapport and developing positive relationships with them. Students not only connect with adults while engaged in learning formally but through more informal activities and in a variety of settings (think of all the interactions happening in the cafeteria, hallways, library, playground, after-school activities, sports events, clubs, and so on).

Fostering meaningful connections is a lifeline. MLs come to school not only to learn a new language, develop literacy in multiple places, and acquire new understandings and skills across the content areas, but they often find themselves negotiating their identities within the framework of a new culture, developing and embracing their multiple language practices, growing friendships or resolving conflicts with their peers, and navigating academic, social, and linguistic expectations set by others or by themselves.

During the pandemic, a sense of stability was shaken to the core for many. With the shuttering of schools, students were uprooted from their everyday lives and forced into unfamiliar routines and isolated learning environments. This change in circumstances greatly impacted MLs' connections and interactions with friends, teachers, and the people they know, care about, and with whom they spend time in school. How did your students fare under these circumstances?

Natural disasters like hurricanes and earthquakes can cause great damage to ecosystems and their inhabitants. Similarly, we have witnessed first-hand and heard from many teachers the extent of the pandemic's disruption to our ecosystems of schools and classrooms. MLs have faced a myriad of new challenges that were amplified by limited access not only to technology devices, instructional materials, or the Internet, but to wraparound support services including access to social workers, school counselors, psychologists, and health care providers as well. Some students experienced significant struggles throughout this time that might have had a long-term impact on their development, including trauma, fear, anxiety, and chronic stress. Beyond these burdens, many MLs and their families also faced food insecurity and shelter insufficiency while others suffered financial struggles and some even abandonment. Although there were rapid support systems put in place in many communities, if MLs felt disconnected and frightened or if they did not have access to (or their families did not know how to access available support services), they might have found themselves further isolated. Connecting with teachers as lifelines to the classroom and school community became even more critical than before!

As COVID-19 positivity rates climbed throughout the United States, many students, families, and educators fell ill. Some students and their families are still experiencing long-term health effects or the loss of those closest to them. Many of our MLs hail from collaborative cultures that embrace multi-generational families living together and supportive communities helping each other. Everyone works together; some have minimal resources, but they make it work. It all changed pretty quickly with an urgent shutdown of all non-emergency facilities including businesses and schools, which created a sense of uncertainty both at home and in school. Many families have faced devastating losses—of work, living space, stability, their perceived sense of "normal," independence, and in so many cases, a loved one.

Learning environments have a profound impact on students; how well they cope, how they maintain their interactions with others, along with the strength and longevity of the connections and relationships they build. To fortify student success in school, we work collectively to build community around them. We here refers to all the people who surround our students, including teachers, administrators, teaching assistants, aides, volunteers, as well as wraparound service providers, such as school-based mental and physical health professionals (school counselors, psychologists, social workers, and nurses).

As we move forward, it must be a priority to create ample opportunities to build and strengthen connections and relationships with students and their families—another important topic that is treated in the latter half of this chapter. Further, we must embrace culturally responsive equitable practices to address what matters most to our students individually and collectively. To accomplish this, let's commit to building a strong rapport and having a clearer understanding of what supports are relevant to and make sense for our students. Let's support teachers and wraparound service providers to develop a better understanding of the diverse cultural backgrounds and belief systems held by MLs and their families as they relate to health, customs, and practices (Lazear, 2015) and focus capacity-building on student-centered practices.

STUDENT PORTRAITS

Luz, Linti, and Joselin used to take the bus to middle school together, chat in the back of the bus, and spend time together after school. But that was before March 2020. Life turned upside down for all of them. When they finally had a chance to talk to the school social worker in person, they opened up about their experiences throughout the pandemic.

Luz expressed how remote learning made her feel more lost and alone. She felt silly asking questions. She missed her friends and didn't feel like she had people around her that were helping her get through it all. Her grandma, who primarily takes care of her, became sick with the virus two months ago and is still in the hospital. She's pretty bad, and the family can't see her. Luz has three little brothers, and she is trying to help them with their schoolwork without really understanding her own. When she was in school, it was easier to talk to her friends, teachers, and sometimes the guidance counselor about what she calls "stuff." She has had to deal with everything on her own. She is happy to be back in school!

Linti was really struggling with math and feeling frustrated a lot. He spoke to a friend about how hard it is to be disconnected from the class and not getting what is going on in math and even in his favorite subject, science! He used to be able to have a quick conversation with a teacher or guidance counselor at school. He felt like everyone was watching him, listening to every word, so he just turned off his camera and mic most of the time. There is no privacy on Google Classroom. He wished he had more opportunities to connect with his teachers. He explained feeling embarrassed about saying something the wrong way or asking a question; he couldn't even have a private conversation with his teacher about everything going on at home. Scary things! He always felt safer at school, but he couldn't leave his apartment to go anywhere for months. He also had to be careful so no one could hear him talking at home. It wasn't safe. If someone overheard him talking, it wouldn't be good. It is good to be back in school but he just feels anxious all the time.

Joselin talked about missing her soccer coach and playing on the field three to four times a week. Ms. S is the one person she has opened up to about her personal life. Joselin lives with an aunt she met when she came to the United States last January. She feels disconnected from her family back home and her new family at school. She lives with five other people in a one-bedroom apartment: her aunt, her aunt's boyfriend, their seven-year-old daughter, and three-year-old twin sons. She shares the living room with her cousin, but quarantine has been really hard. Her aunt expected her to get good grades. She was afraid she would get sick and bring the virus home to everyone—her cousin has autism and asthma. Many times Joselin couldn't concentrate on school because the Wi-Fi is unreliable, and it was hard to find a quiet place to get her work done.

What is waiting for Luz, Linti, and Joselin on the other side of the pandemic? Safe spaces, open doors, and new opportunities to capture their pandemic experiences and move beyond them! These students have stories to tell, histories to write, personal connections to rebuild or strengthen, and the future to focus on! We must be there fully committed to working together in the school community to ensure all students' voices are heard, experiences are validated, and relationships are valued.

Take a moment to reflect on how the pandemic impacted or shaped your relationships and connections by answering the questions that follow:

- *How have your students' relationships and connections been impacted throughout the pandemic?*

- *When we talk with and listen closely to our students about their realities throughout the pandemic, what do they say about safely returning to school? What does returning to face-to-face instruction mean to them?*

- *Consider your own experiences throughout the year and a half or so of the pandemic. How has your experience changed you as a person and teacher? What is important to you personally and professionally, and what are your views for a safe return?*

- *There are many considerations and unforeseeable effects of the pandemic. What strategies have you or will you implement to help students build new connections, strengthen existing ones, and maintain affirming relationships?*

LOOKING BACK, LOOKING AHEAD

Several years before the pandemic hit our shores, more and more MLs began to attend core academic classes with their English-fluent peers. Not all teachers they encountered were proficient in teaching MLs, and at times, little attention was paid to their linguistic, academic, and social-emotional development. Attempts by teachers and students to make connections and build relationships now and again missed the mark. Although some teachers may have participated in professional-learning initiatives designed to get everyone aware and prepared to address issues of equitable learning for and relationship building with MLs, some marginalized students continued to feel even more like outsiders in their own classes. Approaches to remedy these relationship gaps were not and could not be addressed by quick-fix solutions. When one-size-fits-all approaches to building connections and support services were not culturally congruent, they did not help school professionals to fully understand nor address individual needs. In turn, some students developed a lack of trust or connection to their teachers and fellow students, ultimately leaving some MLs feeling isolated and detached.

To honor the unique experiences of our MLs, we need to dig deeply into the systemic inequities facing our students and build capacity among individuals to invest in the "deeper personal, interpersonal, and cultural shifts" (Safir & Dugan, 2021, p. 33). Although many educators do have the best intentions while serving MLs, good intentions alone don't always lead to a positive impact. In the case of MLs', we still find evidence of subtle nuances or sometimes deliberate forms of exclusion that negatively impact how safe, supported, or empowered students feel in their environment. A technical "fix" won't get to the root of such deep-rooted problems. The overarching complexities of equity work require a comprehensive effort implemented over time to address the importance of relational trust and building relationships; it is not just checking off a box to show training on a professional development plan.

During the pandemic, some students functioned within small, dependent units (parents or family members) or interdependent units (siblings, friends, teachers) that allowed them to work together with others to grow academically, linguistically, and socially in their private spaces outside of school. These dependent and interdependent units within the ecosystem of the greater school community (known also as micro-communities) have impacted student connections to and relationships with each other, their teachers, school personnel, and those at home. For example, when learning virtually, certain aspects of students' living spaces were exposed in ways that they never thought would be shared with others—their home was often visible for the whole class to see; they may have had a living situation they hoped no one would ever know; or they may have been embarrassed by their spotty Internet service, repeatedly getting disconnected from their online classes. All these stressors may have created new challenges for students. On the flip side, some students chose to attend school virtually, left their camera on or off, and remained persistently resilient.

Some students isolated by their respective micro-communities lost their connections to the greater school community. As we look ahead to serve our MLs in our brick-and-mortar classrooms, we want to build the capacity of our students to make connections with others in the school community that will foster their growth and development. We need to champion their renewed sense of identities as successful learners, nurture their feelings of belonging, and advocate for their safety and well-being while being physically in school. Our students found ways to continuously connect with their friends through technology via text, gaming, and unstructured online settings such as social media. They connected with teachers and other school personnel through email, text, and virtual meetings and discussions. Yet students will need our continued support to make direct, face-to-face connections and have clear, cogent conversations with one another as they navigate the reality of being back in school.

As we look ahead, we recognize the immense value of fostering relationships with marginalized or minoritized students and promoting their lasting connections to their teachers, peers, and the greater school community. Students who feel connected and develop a sense of belonging have a better chance of succeeding—they are more apt to attend school regularly, are more attentive to their schoolwork, and are more likely to graduate as well as further their education beyond high school. The nurturing relationships that our students need are grounded in perspectives that embrace positive attitudes and beliefs, cultural and linguistic competence, an understanding of the needs and experiences of students, and an understanding of the school environment. In order for students to make meaningful connections with peers and adults, they need intentional systemic supports that honor their individual identities and value relationships in and across all classrooms as well as within the larger school community. The pandemic has served as a catalyst for many educators to rethink relationships in and outside their classrooms and to co-construct new systems to encourage and build productive and intentional connections *with* and *for* our MLs.

Take a moment to reflect on how you plan to build and strengthen relationships with your students and how you support their relationships with others in the school community:

- What do you plan to do to specifically foster relationships with MLs and their families?

- In what specific ways can you give more consideration to individual students and their culturally specific needs inside and outside of the classroom?

- How might you plan to welcome and affirm MLs when they return to brick-and-mortar classrooms?

- What approaches and supports might you employ to help MLs to build, rebuild, and maintain resilient connections with others?

OUR CONNECTED RESPONSIBILITY
TO STUDENTS

What has become clearer to us through this experience? Relationships play a critical role in educating MLs. They did before and during the pandemic, and they will long into the future! Teaching is not "done" to any student and learning does not come from teachers. Learning happens when we are fully engaged *with* others, and teaching may be best conceived as happening *through* relationships (Goodman, 2015). It is all about some of the most essential human qualities and actions we can embrace—caring, communicating, connecting, contributing, cooperating, coproducing, and collaborating with one another. Recognizing how crucial it is to sincerely connect with our students and their families has never been more needed than during a time of crisis.

Ultimately, what will make an immeasurable impact on students is the quality of relationships we nurture in our classroom and school communities: Relationships and interactions between teachers and students, students and students, and educators and families must come first! Through interactions, we get to know each other, learn about each other's strengths, assets, talents, abilities, joys and sorrows, struggles and triumphs. Through relationships, our students learn about themselves and others and the world around them, they develop trust in others, they learn to honor and respect differences, they know the importance of being valued, they are encouraged by praise for their efforts and achievements, and they appreciate guidance and mentorship, and in turn, offer support to others.

Equity for MLs is not a choice; it is the collective responsibility of all educators. As we work together to promote academic success, language and literacy development, and social-emotional well-being, we give careful consideration to representing, supporting, and valuing students while building a strong sense of belonging for all. To strengthen student capacity, we identify the supportive structures students will need as we move forward to embrace individuality and build in opportunities for student engagement outside instructional time in the classroom, school, and community. We structure these authentic opportunities for students to communicate and forge connections across differences to address underlying issues, including inequity, cultural disconnects, and ethnocentrism.

As we return full-time to our brick-and-mortar classrooms, the complexity of students' needs will depend on the impact the pandemic had on them personally as well as the impact it had on their communities both inside and outside school. We will be faced with a once-in-a-lifetime opportunity to create a connected, relationship-rich, new school environment. We advocate for one that focuses on students as individuals through asset-oriented and equitable practices that meet them where they are and best support them as they move forward to navigate unfamiliar territory.

For students to engage in learning, we need to be sensitive to their holistic needs, including emotional, physical, and psychological needs, by creating a caring classroom culture that reflects who they are and encourages them. To further strengthen the classroom culture, we need to recognize the humanity of all our students, instill self-confidence in them, believe in them, rally for their success, and invest in building trusting and long-lasting relationships with them as individuals both inside and outside the classroom.

Pause and reflect on the role collaboration and relationships play in establishing or strengthening the following:

- Fostering equity in your classroom
- Providing challenging and appropriate opportunities to learn
- Building resilience
- Encouraging persistence
- Cultivating positivity and hope
- Inviting reflective practices

You set the example for students' relationships with others through your connections with them and others in the school community. Check in with students daily to see where they are, let them know they are important. Students are a priority, and they need to know you will show up for them every day. For some, you will be the most dependable adult in their life. For others, you will represent a member of a large, extended family of adults who show every day how much they care. You provide challenge and support, listen to them and talk with them, and cheer them on when they need it most. You consider them as you adjust and modify the environment to enhance their learning, be it academic, linguistic, or social-emotional.

To build sustainable and trusting relationships, students need consistency in action and environment throughout the teaching-learning process. Provide opportunities for students to interact and learn to collaborate across racial, ethnic, and linguistic identities through authentic team-building activities, cooperative learning opportunities, and problem- or project-based learning. Such strategies help strengthen bonds naturally when student-to-student interaction is the norm. Authentic experiences allow MLs to be active participants in their own learning and to fully grasp as well as shape what it means to be part of a classroom community. MLs also learn how to engage in collaborative processes without being let down or letting down others. They need to know you will listen to them, take a sincere interest in their lives, and offer honest feedback on what they share with you. All these daily acts of relationship building affirm their worth and contribution to the class and broader school community.

SOCIAL-EMOTIONAL LEARNING IN SUPPORT OF EQUITY

Relationships with students happen in real time every day! Maintaining balance in moments of strife, conflict, fear, and uncertainty along with joy, excitement, ease, and resolution may be tricky. When working with students, circumstances pop up that we expect, and of course, some we do not. We have to be ready for them no matter what comes our way in a responsive, proactive, not reactive manner.

As we move forward, we need to acknowledge we have changed and so have our students. Our initiatives and efforts to support SEL must change with the times as well! Our overarching goal to focus on interactions with others to build, maintain, and strengthen connections, and foster healthy relationships must be expanded. We believe that equity-oriented implementation of SEL will significantly contribute to creating learning environments where all members of the classroom and school community feel valued and affirmed not in spite of but *because of* and *for* their individual talents, gifts, spirits, as well as their cultural and linguistic heritages, backgrounds, and identities.

> *What systems will help us create equity-focused goals?*
>
> Think about the systems you have established in your classroom or are working on more broadly throughout your school. What place or role does equity have in it?
>
> *What did or did not work in the past?*
>
> Use this moment in time to be a springboard into co-constructing more equitable classroom routines, structures, and protocols that affirm students' complex identities and experiences and align SEL to creating inclusive learning environments.

We encourage you and your colleagues to apply a cultural and linguistic (as well as sociopolitical) equity lens and collaboratively review and assess any existing SEL initiatives (whether they are being implemented in a schoolwide, systemic fashion or they are classroom-based protocols that are designed to help foster a healthy mind and body and a healthy community). As noted by CASEL (2021),

> While SEL alone will not solve longstanding and deep-seated inequities in the education system, it can help schools promote understanding, examine biases, reflect on and address the impact of racism, build cross-cultural relationships, and cultivate adult and student practices that close opportunity gaps and create a more inclusive school community. (para 3)

In light of this approach to SEL, collaborate with your colleagues to examine how SEL is interpreted and implemented in your context and establish action steps to address any gaps you may discover:

- Is SEL designed to serve as a mechanism for relationship building and for fostering affirming interactions across racial, ethnic, and linguistic identities and backgrounds?

- Do all MLs and families feel heard and included in SEL initiatives?

- Do all MLs feel cared for and safe to express their own needs and advocate for themselves and others?

- Do MLs feel ownership of not only their academic and linguistic development but their social-emotional growth as well?

- Are all classrooms safe, sacred spaces for MLs to (a) quietly reflect and pause, (b) be heard and affirmed, (c) challenge inequities they notice, (d) lead authentic lives, and (e) initiate change?

Safe and affirming classroom spaces play a key role in building positive relationships between teachers and students as well among students; they can also facilitate students' sustained connections with schooling. Since students' sense of self is paramount to their overall health, recognize how the space you create for them to reflect on their emotions, social interactions, and decision-making processes gives them opportunities to manage their relationships with others. In the broader school community, developing protocols for mindfulness-based, positive behavioral systems challenge students to be their authentic selves. These systems do not focus on punishment and punitive measures. Instead, they approach behavior from a more relevant and culturally sensitive perspective, shifting the narrative and approach to developing relationships with students.

In conjunction with equity-oriented SEL programs and approaches, we also encourage building culturally responsive and sustaining wellness teams to focus on mindfulness, restorative justice, and health. When we combine multiple layers to harness connections, we use a more holistic lens to approach students where health and well-being intersect.

STRATEGIES FOR BUILDING CONNECTIONS IN THE CLASSROOM

While building a healthy learning environment is a complex process, here we suggest five approaches you can use in your classroom to support MLs as we make our way beyond the pandemic:

1. Create and sustain a welcoming, safe, and affirming physical environment for all our students.

2. Get to know your students.

3. Generate authentic opportunities for students to engage with their peers.

4. Provide student mentoring.

5. Incorporate daily mindfulness and self-care practices in the classroom.

CREATE AND SUSTAIN A WELCOMING, SAFE, AND AFFIRMING PHYSICAL ENVIRONMENT FOR ALL OUR STUDENTS

When we provide students with a welcoming, safe, and affirming environment, we lay the foundation for building a community of learners. When students step into your classroom, they should feel welcome and connected to their surroundings. They should also feel a sense of connection to other students and adults who share that space during the school day. The images, quotes, and information posted on the walls should pull them into their environment, unmistakable characteristics that give them a sense of belonging and safety. Within the walls of our classrooms, let's provide pathways for students to engage in opportunities to share information, to see their lives and experiences represented and valued, to both affirm and challenge their thinking, explore commonalities and unique differences, and dialogue with their peers in restorative circles and community meetings. When MLs are engaged this way, students' voices are uplifted as they grow as individuals within the classroom and schoolwide community.

GET TO KNOW YOUR STUDENTS

Building relationships with our students means we need ample time to get to know them. As teachers, we learn about our students through observing their interests, their engagement in learning, their participation in class, and their relationships with their peers, among other things. To create a clearer picture of who our students are and why they act in specific ways, we need to continually seek opportunities to learn about them. Nora Fleming (2020) suggests six ways to increase your knowledge of your students by having them do the following:

- Write reflection essays on the values and principles that guide their lives.

- Create an identity chart with factors that include their ethnicity, gender, education, languages spoken, and so on.

- Develop an inventory of their favorite music, sports, games, food, activities, memories, and family members.

- Produce a passion blog where students write periodically about what they are most passionate about.

- Use digital tools to create a movie or podcast to create a mini-autobiography.

GENERATE AUTHENTIC OPPORTUNITIES FOR STUDENTS TO ENGAGE WITH THEIR PEERS

Let's focus on actively engaging students in a range of challenging yet accessible and meaningful learning opportunities. When learning is authentic, students interact, use their own lived experiences to have discussions, make connections, and build relationships around what they know and have experienced. Learning connected to real-life problems, especially those that students deeply care about, may help them develop critical (Muhammad, 2020) as well as sustainable relationships with their peers, teachers, and other adults in and out of the classroom. Classrooms are governed by mutually agreed-upon norms that students have co-developed with their teachers and peers.

PROVIDE OPPORTUNITIES FOR STUDENT MENTORING

Most of us appreciated the value of strong mentorship in the early days of our teaching practice. Similarly, mentoring students can be paramount to developing self-awareness, fostering personal passions, and promoting student growth. Mentoring provides opportunities for students to work with peers or adults who can support personal and academic goal setting, provide direction for planning toward improvement, and offer guidance on how to recognize and capitalize on individual strengths. Students involved in these opportunities often feel more self-confident, self-reliant, and connected. They also develop a stronger sense of responsibility. Mentors and mentees often set goals and work through the decision-making process in genuine and respectful ways. Students who engage in mentoring programs have demonstrated strong and sustainable connections to others.

INCORPORATE DAILY MINDFULNESS AND SELF-CARE PRACTICES IN THE CLASSROOM

Developing mindfulness supports teachers and students to cultivate awareness, stay in the present moment, and maintain an attitude that is understanding, humane, and compassionate. When we practice mindfulness throughout the day, it gives us a few moments to pause, clear our minds, and rejuvenate ourselves to achieve tasks with clarity. When we teach mindfulness, our students have an opportunity to get in touch with their thoughts and feelings. It can promote self-care for our students and also allows us time for our own personal care as well. Our students need to learn this very important skill to lower their stress and anxiety—and adults need it, too! When mindfulness practices become routine for us (both students and teachers), we are able to connect with ourselves, and we are better able to connect with others.

Pause for a moment and reflect on additional ways you can build a supportive classroom environment. The more time we spend getting to know our students and interacting with them, the more they will know that we care about who they are; in turn, they will learn to trust more and better engage in the learning process.

STRATEGIES FOR BUILDING CONNECTIONS BEYOND THE CLASSROOM

We are reminded of the frequently quoted proverb to underscore the importance of reaching and engaging the entire community in MLs' education: *You need a village to raise a child.* When we see, hear, and recognize our MLs' immediate and extended families as a resource, we reach out to them, we partner with them, and we invite them to help make important decisions about their children's academic, linguistic, and social-emotional growth. On the other hand, when families see the school as a place to trust, critical community relationships are forged. Joyce Epstein and colleagues (2019) were the first to refer to this powerful phenomena right before the pandemic as *family-like schools*—where educators and all school personnel know and value children for who they are, just like their own families, parents, caregivers, and relatives would—and *school-like families*—who acknowledge their role and responsibility to support their children's education to the best of their ability by working in collaboration with educators and all others providing support services within the school system. As we return to school, let's commit to building or rediscovering relationships that foster family-like schools and school-like families.

In family-like schools, let's make a commitment to celebrating each child's gift, talent, and spirit as loving, caring families do. Similarly, in school-like families, let's engage parents in authentic, extended learning opportunities, such as place-based project-based learning, family oral histories, and so on. These dynamic relationships are designed to lead to increased self-confidence for students, stronger connections to school life, more engaged families, and multiple sources of support for the multilingual learner (Cohan et al., 2020). How do we start to make or strengthen connections between schools and families?

KEY STRATEGIES TO CONSIDER

- Seek input from parents when designing culturally and linguistically responsive and sustaining curriculum and instruction for their children.

- Encourage parents to share how their children learn best.

- Embrace the rich linguistic, literacy, and cultural experiences and assets.

- Ensure that the community becomes a core source of information and support.

- Recruit liaisons with strong community connections, who are fluent in the language and culture of the people in the community and are trusted by all.

As families feel more confident in their roles in the school community, we must continue to prioritize family engagement and seek opportunities for schools to directly connect with students and families. Some practices for sustaining family engagement include the following:

- Providing free workshops (in multiple languages) for parents to learn about the services offered both within and outside the school.

- Offering free adult classes to support language learning.

- Providing parents with native language resources to support them in advocating for their children's education, mental health, and social-emotional well-being.

- Opening libraries in the buildings to give greater access to literacy resources.

In the best cases, our schools can serve as vital hubs for resourcing families and the surrounding community. Proactively cultivating connections will allow students and families to build agency by being more autonomous as they foster and sustain relationships with those around them. If you reach a point where students' needs are outside your comfort zone or they need a different type of support, reach out to the school community that provides the wraparound services (such as mental health, counseling, medical resources, and so on). This communicative environment is beneficial for our MLs and their families and helps them feel part of the greater school community. We all grow from these practices.

Reflect on how we engage with our students and their families, and provide opportunities to connect with them and the greater school community:

- In what ways do you cultivate connections with students, families, wraparound service providers, and the community beyond your classroom walls?

- What support systems does your school or district have in place to field student and family questions about the availability of resources pertaining to mental health and well-being?

- What strategies ensure equity and availability of access to technology and other resources for your students, their families, and the community in the classroom and schoolwide environments?

TALK WITH AND LISTEN TO YOUR STUDENTS

Imagine a space in your classroom where you can share stories and learn more about your students on a personal level—a space where you share a little of your own story. When we share our stories, we drop our defenses and give a little part of ourselves. As a result, we lay the foundation for others to share. Storytelling is one way that you and your students can start to build trust—trust on a level beyond learning; it's personal. Take a moment to settle in and close the outside world. Let the students know it's just you and them. They are safe. They start to trust; they start to open up, and it becomes okay for them to share a little of their story. It feels a little risky at first, but you shared a little of yourself, and that means something to them. It shows the human side of you; it levels the playing field. They feel like people with voices, and they share. They share because you make them feel like it matters. Their voices matter; it validates them in ways you may not realize. The process begins to give students confidence as they build trust and break down their walls. They feel connected and mutually respected in this space. They feel important.

Our students have experienced disconnect, isolation, loss, and so much more throughout the last year. Despite such negative consequences, many have also grown in ways that we don't typically measure. When we listen closely, we learn the depth of their struggle and perseverance throughout their lives and more recently, the pandemic. Their voices depict the moments, and these moments capture the essence of their experiences. They offer us an opportunity to empathize, observe, and provide validation of their experiences as we return to school, a new normal that pushes the status quo. Hear them, imagine your own students' voices, gain some insights into the microcosms of their stories. Help them understand and feel how much they matter.

EQUITY IN ACTION

Kristina Robertson, an English learner program administrator for Roseville Public Schools in a small suburban district bordering St. Paul, Minnesota, shared with us her district's initiative.

Anyone who has worked with MLs is familiar with the language barriers inherent in our education systems. Providing language access is a high-leverage equity action that can increase student well-being and academic achievement. I address language barriers with the help of a talented cultural liaison team and by providing teachers direct access to an easy interpreter app. The combination of support from a culturally and linguistically diverse cultural liaison team along with direct teacher communication in over 80 languages has been imperative to educational success during the COVID pandemic.

Our district leadership has made a strong commitment to our multilingual/ multicultural families. We have 16 cultural liaisons representing five languages,

African American and Native American communities in a district with an enrollment of 7,500. Cultural liaisons are the heart of our connection and partnership with students, families, and communities. Our bilingual cultural liaisons are a major conduit for families to share concerns, ask questions, and get support when they are struggling. Most families have cultural liaisons on speed dial, and communication by phone is key due to the oral cultural component. Many cultural liaisons have worked for our district longer than five years, and the relationships they built with families and students go deep.

District leaders and educators really experienced the benefits of these relationships when immigration law changes in 2016 led to increased deportations and anti-Muslim media campaigns. Our Latin and Somali communities were anxious, and the cultural liaisons worked tirelessly fielding student and family questions and connecting them with social workers and community resources to ensure a network of support. They also collaborated with district leaders to develop an immigrant support guidance document to inform teachers, social workers, and administrators on appropriate responses to student anxiety around immigration issues and provided letter-of-support templates for families involved in deportation proceedings. This work was crucial to addressing the social-emotional needs of the Latin and Somali communities by sending the message that "All are welcome here" and increasing staff awareness of racism and complex immigration law. All the cultural liaisons are trained circle facilitators, who invite students to share their stories and experiences in a safe space in their native language. This is a very important pressure release valve for multicultural teens who are navigating multiple socio-cultural norms from their home language and culture, U.S. English school and teen culture, and their own evolving cultural identity.

As we entered the pandemic year, we experienced language and cultural barriers on a larger scale. Our cultural liaison team was overwhelmed and not familiar with all the technology needed for students to access learning. They worked long hours helping families get Wi-Fi connections, iPad, and email accounts. With approximately 2,000 students who speak a language other than English, it was clear that ALL staff needed to be able to communicate directly with multilingual families. In fall 2019, the district began using an interpreter app from Dialog One that is installed on staff iPads, (or staff can add it to their own phone), which allows them to push a button and instantly connect with an interpreter in 80+ languages and make a direct connection with parents/guardians. Staff were anxious about using the interpreter app in the beginning, and I suggested they make practice calls to the interpreter line so they could experience how easy it was to get an interpreter. Once the pandemic hit, the staff pushed aside any anxiety and began making direct calls to multilingual families to check in. Many teachers have reported that they have developed stronger relationships with parents that they didn't know that well prior to the pandemic. Teachers share stories of weekly chats with some parents and sending bilingual messages with the SeeSaw and Talking Points apps. The partnership they've formed to ensure student success is fostered by language access and digital tools.

All parents want their children to be successful, and for too long, many multilingual families have been in the dark due to a text-heavy, Internet-based, English district communication system. The pandemic highlighted the inequities multilingual families *experience as districts scrambled to find ways to communicate important information in multiple languages in writing and orally. If there is one positive from this pandemic, it will be the ongoing commitment by leaders and educators partnering with multilingual families to deepen their understanding of cultural assets and collaborate for student success.*

PARTING THOUGHTS

Encouraging MLs to cultivate relationships in safe, culturally responsive, and supportive school environments is paramount as we move beyond the pandemic to return to physical and hybrid classroom settings. Strong connections to teachers and wraparound service providers help MLs learn how to overcome adversity and trauma by breaking down barriers and developing coping mechanisms to overcome and respond to changes through proactive and reflective approaches. Through their relationships, students learn how to trust themselves and the adults around them. They learn to become confident, resilient, and independent individuals who understand when to seek out the support systems they need to navigate their personal environments.

Reflections and Actions

1. We compared the connections and relationships in the classroom and the greater school community to an ecosystem. In what ways does this metaphor support the intricate and unique relationships we build with our students? What approaches can you use in your classroom to support all students?

2. How do you build equitable connections with students to ensure they feel seen, heard, and valued in your classroom? How do you foster these relationships with families and wraparound service providers?

3. What are your core beliefs, ideas, and practices that recognize student promise and potential? How do you hold students accountable in their environment while maintaining culturally sensitive, compassionate, and caring connections?

4. What opportunities are provided for MLs and their families to connect with each other and other members of the larger school community?

5. Students' sense of self is paramount to their overall health and well-being. How do you provide them with authentic opportunities to engage with others and develop a stronger sense of self?

6. We offered a range of strategies for building connections in and beyond the classroom. Critically review and evaluate these strategies and make plans to implement the ones most applicable to your context.

Key Resources

Immigrant Connections:

https://www.immigrantsrefugeesandschools.org/

Bridging Refugee Youth and Children's Services (BRYCS):

https://brycs.org/

Understood (a nonprofit organization to help shape the world for difference):

https://www.understood.org/en/school-learning/for-educators/partnering-with-families/6-strategies-for-partnering-with-families-of-english-language-learners

CASEL (A Collaborative for Academic, Social, and Emotional Learning):

www.casel.org

References and Further Reading

Acevedo, E. (2020). *Clap when you land*. Harper Teen.

Aguilar, E. (2021). *Coaching for equity; Conversations that change practice*. Jossey-Bass.

ASCD. (2021). *Whole child*. http://www.ascd.org/whole-child.aspx

Bishop, S. R. (1990). Mirrors, windows, and sliding glass doors. *Perspectives, 1*(3), ix–xi.

Blankstein, A. M., Cole, R. W., & Houston, P.D. (Eds.). (2007). *Engaging every learner*. Corwin.

Boykin, A. W., & Noguera, P. (2011). *Creating the opportunity to learn*. Corwin.

Brown, D. (2021). *A shot in the arm!: Big ideas that changed the world #3*. Amulet Books.

Bunch, G. C., & Walqui, A. (2019). Educating English learners in the 21st century. In A. Walqui & G. C. Bunch (Eds.), *Amplifying the curriculum: Designing quality learning opportunities for English learners* (pp. 1–20). Teachers College Press.

Calderón, M. E., Dove, M. G., Staehr Fenner, D., Gottlieb, M., Honigsfeld, A., Ward Singer, T., Slakk, S., Soto, I., & Zacarian, D. (2020). *Breaking down the wall: Essential shifts for English learners' success*. Corwin.

CASEL. (2019). *SEL 3 signature practices playbook: A tool that supports systemic social and emotional learning.* https://schoolguide.casel.org/uploads/2018/12/CASEL_SEL-3-Signature-Practices-Playbook-V3.pdf

CASEL. (2021). *Equity and SEL*. https://schoolguide.casel.org/what-is-sel/equity-and-sel/

Center for Public Education. (2016). *Educational equity: What does it mean? How do we know when we reach it?* https://www.nsba.org/-/media/nsba/file/cpe-educational-equity-research-brief-january-2016.

Chamot, A. U., & O'Malley, J. M. (1986). *A cognitive academic language approach: An ESL content-based curriculum*. National Clearing House for Bilingual Education.

Cohan, A., Honigsfeld, A., & Dove, M. G. (2020). *Team up, speak up, fire up!: Educators and the community working together to support English learners*. ASCD.

Cummins, J., & Early, M. (Eds.). (2011). *Identity texts: The collaborative creation of power in multilingual schools*. Trentham Books.

Donohoo, J. (2017). *Collective efficacy: How educators' beliefs impact student learning*. Corwin.

Echevarría, J., Vogt, M. E., & Short, D. J. (2000). *Making content comprehensible for English learners: The SIOP model*. Allyn and Bacon.

Education and Justice Research and Organizing Collaborative (EJ-ROC). (2021). *Culturally responsive curriculum scorecard*. https://steinhardt.nyu.edu/metrocenter/ejroc/culturally-responsive-curriculum-scorecards

Epstein, J. L., Sanders, M. G., Sheldon, S. B., Simon, B. S., Salinas, K. C., Jansorn, N. Z., Van Voorhis, F. L., Martin, C. L., Thomas, B G., Greenfeld, M. D., Hutchins, D. J., & Williams, K. J. (2019). *School, family, and community partnerships: Your handbook for action* (4th ed.). Corwin.

Fisher, D., Frey, N., & Hattie, J. (2017). *Teaching literacy in the visible learning classroom: K-5 companion for visible learning for literacy*. Corwin.

Fleming, N. (2020). *6 exercises to get to know your students better-and increase their engagement*. https://www.edutopia.org/article/6-exercises-get-know-your-students-better-and-increase-their-engagement

García, O., & Wei, L. (2014). *Translanguaging: Language, bilingualism and education*. Springer.

Garrett, C. (2021). Relevant curriculum is equitable curriculum. *Educational Leadership, 78*(6), 48–53.

Goleman, D., & Senge, P. (2014). *The triple focus: A new approach to education*. More Than Sound.

Goodman, S. (2015). *The importance of teaching through relationships*. https://www.edutopia.org/blog/importance-teaching-through-relationships-stacey-goodman

Hammond, Z. (2015). *Culturally responsive teaching and the brain*. Corwin.

Hartocollis, A. (2021, March 18). 'When a normal life stopped': College essays reflect a turbulent year. *The New York Times*, p. A21. https://www.nytimes.com/2021/03/17/us/covid-college-admissions.html?searchResultPosition=1

Kibler, A., Valdés, G., & Walqui, A. (Eds.) (2021). *Reconceptualizing the role of critical dialogue in*

American classrooms: Promoting equity through dialogic education. Routledge.

Krathwol, D. R. (2002). A revision of Bloom's taxonomy: An overview. *Theory into Practice, 41*(4), 212–218.

Kraus, R., & Aruego, J. (1999). *Leo the late bloomer.* HarperCollins.

Law, N., & Robertson, R. (2021, March 18). *Assessing the impact of equity work.* [Equity Webinar Series: Session 2]. Arizona State Department.

Lazear, K. (2015). Why cultural competence is one of wraparound's greatest strengths and most persistent challenges. *The TA Telescope, 1*(2), 1–9. https://nwi.pdx.edu/pdf/CulturalCompetenceAndWrap.pdf

Love, B. (2020). *Teachers, we cannot go back to the way things were.* https://www.edweek.org/leadership/opinion-teachers-we-cannot-go-back-to-the-way-things-were/2020/04

MacDonald, R., Crowther, D., Braaten, M., Binder, W., Chien, J., Dassler, T., Shelton, T., & Wilfrid, J. (2020). *Design principles for engaging multilingual learners in three-dimensional science* (WCER Working Paper No. 2020-1). University of Wisconsin–Madison, Wisconsin Center for Education Research. http://www.wcer.wisc.edu/publications/working-papers

Moll, L. C., Amanti, C., Neff, D., & Gonzalez, N. (1992). Funds of knowledge for teaching: Using a qualitative approach to connect homes and classrooms. *Theory into Practice, 31*(2), 132–141. https://doi.org/10.1080/00405849209543534

Muhammad, G. (2020). *Cultivating genius: An equity framework for culturally and historically responsive literacy.* Scholastic.

Muhammad, I., & Ali, S. K. (2019). *The proudest blue: A story of hijab and family.* Little, Brown and Company.

National Equity Project. (n.d.). *Focal students: Equity in the classroom.* https://www.nationalequityproject.org/webinar-recordings

Nordmeyer, J., Boals, T., MacDonald, R., & Westerlund, R. (2021). What does equity really mean for multilingual learners? *Educational Leadership, 78*(6), 60–65.

Oluo, J. (2019). *So you want to talk about race.* Seal Press.

O'Neill, P. T. (n.d.). *And how are the children?* https://www.uua.org/worship/words/reading/and-how-are-the-children

Ottow, S. B. (2019). *The language lens for content classrooms: A guide for K-12 teachers of English and academic language learners.* LSI.

Roy, A. (2020). *The pandemic is a portal.* https://www.ft.com/content/10d8f5e8-74eb-11ea-95fe-fcd274e920ca

Rues, K. (2021, April 5). Students are struggling: They're asking us to slow down and focus on relationships. *EdSurge.* https://www.edsurge.com/news/2021-04-05-students-are-struggling-they-re-asking-us-to-slow-down-and-focus-on-relationships

Safir, S., & Dugan, J., with Wilson, C. (2021). *Street data: A next-generation model for equity, pedagogy, and school transformation.* Corwin.

Simmons, D. (2021). Why SEL alone isn't enough. *Educational Leadership, 78*(6), 30–34.

Sleeter, C. E., & Carmona, J. F. (2017). *Un-standardizing curriculum: Multicultural teaching in the standards-based classroom.* Teachers College Press.

Smith, D., Frey, N., Pumpian, I., & Fisher, D. (2017). *Building equity: Policies and practices to empower all learners.* ASCD.

Snyder, S., & Staehr Fenner, D. (2021). *Culturally responsive teaching for multilingual learners: Tools for equity.* Corwin.

Snyder, T. T. (2020). *What shall we do about the children after the pandemic?* https://portside.org/2020-12-31/what-shall-we-do-about-children-after-pandemic

Soland, J., & Sandilos, L. E. (2021). English language learners, self-efficacy, and the achievement gap: Understanding the relationship between academic and social-emotional growth. *Journal of Education for Students Placed at Risk, 26*(1), 20–44. https://doi.org/10.1080/10824669.2020.1787171

Soto-Hinman, I., & Hetzel, J. (2009). *The literacy gap: Bridge-building strategies for English language learners and standard English learners.* Corwin.

Stone, N. (2017). *Dear Martin.* Crown Publishing Group.

Walqui, A. (2020). *Improving education for English learners: Q&A with Aída Walqui.* https://www.wested.org/rd_alert_online/education-for-english-learners-aida-walqui/#

White, N. J. (1944). I taught them all. *The Clearing House: A Journal of Educational Strategies, Issues and Ideas, 19*(2), 111. https://doi.org/10.1080/00098655.1944.11473980

WIDA. (2020). *WIDA English Language Development Standards Framework, 2020 edition: Kindergarten–Grade 12.* https://wida.wisc.edu/sites/default/files/resource/WIDA-ELD-Standards-Framework-2020.pdf

Yilmaz, K. (2011). The cognitive perspective on learning: Its theoretical underpinnings and implications for classroom practices. *Clearing House: A Journal of Educational Strategies, Issues and Ideas, 84*(5), 204–212.

Zacarian, D., Alvarez-Ortiz, L., & Haynes, J. (2017). *Teaching to strengths: Supporting students living with trauma, violence, and chronic stress.* ASCD.

Zacarian, D., Calderon, M. E., & Gottlieb, M. (2021). *Beyond crises: Overcoming linguistic and cultural inequities in communities, schools, and classrooms.* Corwin.

Index

A SAGE Publishing Company

CORWIN HAS ONE MISSION: to enhance education through intentional professional learning.

We build long-term relationships with our authors, educators, clients, and associations who partner with us to develop and continuously improve the best evidence-based practices that establish and support lifelong learning.

Solutions YOU WANT | Experts YOU TRUST | Results YOU NEED

EVENTS

>>> INSTITUTES

Corwin Institutes provide large regional events where educators collaborate with peers and learn from industry experts. Prepare to be recharged and motivated!

corwin.com/institutes

ON-SITE PD

>>> ON-SITE PROFESSIONAL LEARNING

Corwin on-site PD is delivered through high-energy keynotes, practical workshops, and custom coaching services designed to support knowledge development and implementation.

corwin.com/pd

>>> PROFESSIONAL DEVELOPMENT RESOURCE CENTER

The PD Resource Center provides school and district PD facilitators with the tools and resources needed to deliver effective PD.

corwin.com/pdrc

ONLINE

>>> ADVANCE

Designed for K–12 teachers, Advance offers a range of online learning options that can qualify for graduate-level credit and apply toward license renewal.

corwin.com/advance

Contact a PD Advisor at (800) 831-6640 or visit www.corwin.com for more information